SHE'S NOT
HERSELF

PRAISE FOR *SHE'S NOT HERSELF*
AND LINDA APPLEMAN SHAPIRO

"An honest and compelling story by a brave and gifted writer." ~ **Wally Lamb**, author of *She's Come Undone* and *I Know This Much Is True*; winner of the National Alliance for the Mentally Ill's Kenneth Johnson Award for the anti-stigmatization of mental illness

"A story that applies to us all—truthful, carefully crafted, and created with a clear-eyed affection." ~ **David Watts**, MD, poet, writer, musician, NPR commentator

"A riveting tale wrapped in elegant prose. A very human story— one of hope and perseverance that resonates deeply within the soul." ~ **Peggy Sanders**, retired journalist, award-winning author

"Lyrical and powerful in its use of story telling to subvert secrets and create new selfhood, this is a beautifully written memoir in the tradition of *Eat Pray Love*, *Swallow The Ocean*, *Three Little Words*, or *Lucky Her Last Death*." ~ **Rachel Fichter**, editor-at-large

"For Shapiro's amazing recall and deep penetration into her past, this memoir reminds me of *Remembrance of Things Past*, and for its ease of readability, *A Tree Grows in Brooklyn*." ~ **P. Topping**, linguist

"Inspiring and eloquent...vividly captures the cultural context of an immigrant family living with the trauma of mental illness and its effect on all family relationships." ~ **Joseph Giordano**, LCSW, co-editor, *Ethnicity and Family Therapy*

"A compelling tale of human tragedy and triumph told with empathy and love, without sentimentality...offering a sense of awe for the human spirit." ~ **Pamposh Dhar**, founder of the Terataii Reiki and Counseling Centre, Singapore, Reiki healer, teacher, counselor, blogger

"One feels privileged to share each of the traumas that Shapiro, her mother, and her mother before her had to endure. As to the writing, such complete recall is preserved for all time. Look to your laurels, Marcel Proust." ~ **Frederick Rolf**, actor, director, co-author, translator, *Berlin-Shanghai, New York: My Family's Flight From Hitler*

"Not another 'woe is me' account of dysfunction, but rather a heroic account of mastery and grace, which the general reading public as well as students and professionals will benefit from reading." ~ **Roberta Temes**, PhD, author of several books, including *Learning How to Write a Memoir in Thirty Days*

"With extraordinary insight and honesty, Shapiro shares with us her journey from infinite pain to knowledge, healing, and forgiveness without a trace of melodrama. A truly inspiring read!" ~ **R. G. Sterling**, musician, educator

"Shapiro's moving, meaningful, and beautifully written memoir will resonate with anyone struggling to understand and accept a loved one's illness and its effects on all family members." ~ **Sandra Beckwith**, award-winning publicist, speaker, coach, author

"Writing honestly about her experiences as the daughter of a mother with mental illness...coping with the confusion of mood swings...her struggles to understand and the stress of keeping it all a secret...make for an enlightening and ultimately therapeutic read." ~ **Randye Kaye**, radio host, actress, author of *Ben Behind His Voices: One Family's Journey from the Chaos of Schizophrenia to Hope*

SHE'S NOT HERSELF

A PSYCHOTHERAPIST'S JOURNEY INTO AND BEYOND HER MOTHER'S MENTAL ILLNESS

LINDA APPLEMAN SHAPIRO

Dream *of* Things
Downers Grove Illinois USA
dreamofthings.com

Publisher's Cataloging-in-Publication data:

Shapiro, Linda Appleman.

    She's not herself : a psychotherapist's journey into and beyond her mother's mental illness / Linda Appleman Shapiro.

    p. cm.

    ISBN 9780988439078

1. Shapiro, Linda Appleman. 2. Shapiro, Linda Appleman --Family. 3. Children of the mentally ill. 4. Mentally ill --Family relationships. 4. Psychotherapist --United States --Biography. I. Title.

RC455.4 .F3 S46 2014

362.2/0422/092 --dc23   2014945080

Book design: Susan Veach

Some of the content of *She's Not Herself* was previously published in *Four Rooms, Upstairs* by Linda Appleman Shapiro (Cold Tree Press, 2007). Some names have been changed to protect the privacy of individuals.

For Mother,
who I trust knows I am honoring her as I share our story

In memory of Lori Blank Davis

A dear friend whose life exemplified
love, loyalty, and extraordinary courage

"If no one is home, then someone is missing.
So you grieve."

–Wally Lamb
I Know This Much is True

"The real voyage of discovery consists
not in seeking new landscapes but in having new eyes."

–Marcel Proust
Remembrance of Things Past

CONTENTS

FOREWORD

In the summer of 2005, a group of writers gathered on the campus of Sarah Lawrence College in New York, bringing their words and their hopes for a clear voice to speak them. They shared a common belief that out of the experience of illness and healing there would come great literature, a literature arising from the very core of human existence. The occasion was the *Writing the Medical Experience* Summer Conference and Workshops.

Stories and poems have, throughout history, embodied the codes we need to live well in a difficult world, wisdoms earned from confronting life with the writerly tools of close observation and the power that words have to show us a path. As such this body of knowledge accomplishes Horace's dictum: *Good authors simply delight. The great ones mix the useful with the sweet.*

One of our participants at this conference was Linda Appleman Shapiro. She brought as material for her writing her personal struggles against the intrusion and pain of her mother's mental illness and the first efforts she'd made to transform this chaos into literature. As a result, we now have this wonderful book.

It is not easy to rotate the investigative eye inward, nor is it easy to see clearly the turmoil that results from traumas we endure. The very process of enduring often covers over the details of injury and mutes the emotional currents it generates. Self-analysis becomes impaired by the very manner in which we struggle to protect ourselves. Yet literature demands we set aside our fears and our protections in order to address the meat of life. That is both the process of enlightenment and of healing. It takes courage and a very sharp pencil.

In *She's Not Herself*, Linda brings her talents as a psychotherapist—her courage to expose mental and emotional pain—and the power that writing has to demand a candid rendering of the truth. As always when stories are truthful, carefully crafted, and created with a clear-eyed affection for their topic, they will apply to us all.

DAVID WATTS

David Watts, M.D., is a renowned endocrinologist/internal medicine physician and a clinical professor of medicine at the University of California San Francisco. A true Renaissance man, he is also an award-winning author and poet, a teacher and workshop leader, a commentator for National Public Radio, and a classically trained musician.

WITH SPECIAL THANKS TO:

My extraordinary publisher, Mike O'Mary of Dream of Things, whose belief in my memoir and whose many thoughtful suggestions made this book possible. To Amy Merrick, editor, whose insightful understanding of my story and exceptionally professional skills were a source of encouragement throughout our work together. A special thanks, as well, to author Madeline Sharples for introducing me to Dream of Things.

My brother, Herb, who lovingly helped me to survive my earliest years.

My life-long friends, Stephanie Alt, June C. Berry, Lavinia Hall, Marion and Sam Kriegel, Barbara and David November, Veronica Mary and Frederick Rolf for their unconditional love, their honesty, and the sustenance they have always provided.

My exceptional mentors, Ruth Hersh, Dr. Nina Evans, and Joanne Mortimer.

My fellow students, particularly Brian Malloy, Mary Hower, and Pamela Hull from David Watts' writing workshop, *Writing from the Medical Experience* at Sarah Lawrence College. Their genuine excitement about my writing encouraged me to complete what had been a work in progress.

To the various authors and editors throughout my journey who further educated me about the writing process—especially to authors Pat Carr and Elizabeth Gold, and editors Rachel Fichter and Claire Gerus. Their piercing questions always led me to places I had not yet explored. I am extremely grateful to each of them.

My daughter Keren who, from the moment I decided to write this memoir, offered much needed loving care and encouragement at every turn.

My daughter Mia whose awareness of a reader's need for visual as well as emotional truths inspired me to create dialogue, people, and places in ways that would never have occurred to me without her guidance.

My husband, George, for his expert advice and unconditional love—not only during this project but throughout our forty-six years together.

And a special mention to my grandson Eric and granddaughter Sophie who I hope will read this memoir one day and, in so doing, learn more about their grandmother, their extended family history, and, perhaps, themselves.

SHE'S NOT
HERSELF

CHAPTER 1
MAKE MOTHER HAPPY

Mother didn't read to me. She told me stories—stories that distracted her from her chores and seemed to give her energy. I remember all of them, even the ones I heard before I was old enough to understand.

Since I seldom had an appetite as a young child, Mother told me many of her stories at dinnertime to distract me so I would eat. Most were of her childhood in Russia, and her favorite one—the one I thought gave her the most pleasure, given her broad, carefree smile as she told it—explained why I was conceived.

She began most meals serving half a grapefruit, its sections cut perfectly with her serrated knife, and she started the story the same way each time. She always spoke to me in English, her sentences retaining hints of Yiddish and Russian. "When my sister Fannie's husband, Joe, my favorite brother in-law, died unexpectedly—here, take a little spoonful of the grapefruit—I took it very hard. I was besides myself, *mamaleh*. He was my number one supporter, the only person in the whole family who gave me hope."

A fleeting smile brightened her face, and then vanished. "Just another piece," she urged, bringing the food to my lips. "He always told me, 'Miriam, you're so beautiful. You have so much to live for. Take yourself to the boardwalk. Sit on a bench facing the beach and the ocean. Let the sun shine on you. It'll be a tonic. I promise. You'll feel better.' And he was right. To look at the ocean and watch the waves, with the warm sun on my cheeks, was better than medicine."

When she paused, her eyes grew teary. I felt a familiar knot twisting in my stomach as I sensed that she was no longer talking to me but to herself.

"One day," she began, "your Uncle Joe, he was dead—gone forever. Just like my mama and *tateh*." She lifted her fork. "All right, now we'll start with a little fish and some nice carrots."

She went on, her tone gaining a lilt, her eyes twinkling again. "So, Dr. Andrews—he was the same doctor who delivered your brother, Herbie, six years earlier, and he knew me and knew my problems—he told me, 'Now's the time to have a baby, Miriam. If you take care of a baby, your mind won't be on your sadness. It will be good for you, cheer you up.'

"Here, mamaleh," she urged, "you're almost finished. Just another spoonful of the carrots."

She looked at me with a coy expression and blushed. "Well, that's all your father had to hear. One, two, three, boom! I was pregnant. This time it wasn't like with your brother, when I had a terrible pregnancy. But we don't need to talk about that now."

Her words often evoked anxiety, but I never doubted her love for me. I listened and occasionally nodded.

"The nine months with you," she continued, "they flew by.

Before I knew it, you were here. The day was filled with sunshine, and you came out perfect. Now, just take this one last piece." She offered a final serving of carrots. "You were round and soft and beautiful. God gave me my own sweet little mamaleh. Just like a doll you were. And Dr. Andrews, he was right. You made me happy. You always make me happy. Especially," she added, "when you finish what's on your plate."

She paused, then added: "Protecting myself, I wasn't always so good at. But you were a baby, and you I could protect."

After my last bite, she hugged me. I leaned into her full breasts, her warm body at my side, and was comforted having her near me. The message was clear: Mother needed me to eat. I needed to make her happy.

Eventually, I knew it all by heart, word for word. I seldom remembered what I ate, though, or how the food tasted. What was important was that Mother looked happy because my plate was empty. She glanced at my plate and smiled.

"Isn't that a wonderful story?" She never waited for an answer. I sat there full but burdened, not understanding why.

What I *did* know was that my problem with food was the one topic of conversation that my parents shared with everyone. Mother called it a *shandeh*, a shame, and Father angrily challenged anyone who suggested a solution.

"You try," he said. "She zippers her mouth shut. I never seen such a thing. A child with no appetite!"

"The issue" with food, as Mother later referred to it, was resolved a few years later when I was eight. Dr. Andrews suggested I see an allergist, and after tests proved his hunch accurate, the doctor assured Mother that I'd eat once my nasal passages weren't stuffed. After a year of twice-weekly allergy injections, I gained ten pounds and grew three inches. The cure, though, came with a painful loss. I never again had that special feeling of being so needed and cared for, with Mother seated nearby, nurturing me with food and feeding me stories.

On Tuesdays, she served me baby lamb chops, a baked potato, and Del Monte's peas and carrots, and then ate my leftovers. "Lamb is expensive," she reminded me. "But for my mamaleh, it's worth every penny if she eats it."

Mother's devotion was to her family, never to herself. The only full meal I ever saw her eat was breakfast: a soft-boiled egg in an egg cup, a slice of toast with butter, Postum with milk and no sugar. I never saw her eat with Herbie or Father, so I assumed she just nibbled on food while she was preparing our meals or ate leftovers while doing the dishes. The one exception was Fridays, when we'd at least attempt to sit together for our *Shabbat* dinner.

When I finished eating each evening, Mother would call Herbie to the table, and because I idolized my big brother, I remained in the kitchen just to be with him. He'd pinch my cheeks when he saw me and always said, "They're just so cute!"

Herbie would always compliment Mother's cooking, giving her special thanks when she served something he loved. He often used the word, stretching it out to "lo-oove," especially when he referred to Mother's homemade chicken soup or applesauce, or when she bought him whatever fruits were in season. Mother said that because he was athletic, he was neither too thin nor too fat. "He's just right. Herbie's perfect," she concluded.

I thought he was perfect because he exuded enthusiasm. His contagious energy made me feel more alive, despite the fact that he was out of the house more than he was in it. As eager as he was to be pleasant when he was home, he was just as eager to leave.

Before Father came home from work, and after Mother served each of us, Herbie would rush out to play with his friends. Mother would then ask me to help her "doll up," while she gave herself "a one-two-three quick scrub" with Ivory soap and dusted talcum powder all over her body.

"This is what ladies do for their husbands," she explained. "They tidy up before their men come home from work. They fix their hair and put on a little makeup."

I would eagerly help her snap her long brassiere shut before she hooked it to her girdle. When the corset was assembled, she smiled at herself in the hallway mirror and said, "Now my tired back will feel less achy, and I'll be able to stand up straight to serve your Papa."

I loved that smell of Ivory soap, along with the almond scent of Jergens lotion on her hands and the sweet aroma of her auburn curls. Mesmerized, I'd watch as she'd dab on her Revlon pressed powder, apply her ruby-red lipstick, and then use her small, Woolworth's ten-cent pencil to meticulously fill in the tiny gaps in her delicately arched eyebrows.

As I looked at her smooth, wrinkle-free face, I considered my mother to be a woman of absolute beauty.

There were other times, though, when my mother's face would change beyond recognition. Mother and Father would argue about things I didn't understand while I sat silently, too timid to speak, never knowing what to do or what to ask. During those times, the mother I adored was lost to me, her gentle voice shrill, her soft pink cheeks ghostly white.

All Father would say was, "Your mother, she's not herself these days." Perhaps he had no words to explain her illness to himself, let alone to a child of five. Yet if she wasn't herself, who was she?

Most nights, Father would come home around six o'clock, and I listened for the sound of his keys jingling as he opened the door. He would stop to rest at the top of the stairway, kiss Mother on the cheek, and then kiss Herbie and me. This nightly ritual also included taking his jacket off, hanging it up in his closet, and washing his hands in the bathroom, before finally sitting down alone at the head of the kitchen table.

"It's good for him to eat by himself," Mother told Herbie and me after we had eaten. "He deserves to eat in peace."

That was our cue to leave the table. I usually went into my room while Father ate, but sometimes I walked into the living room, where I'd color in one of my coloring books. As I sat on the floor, the coloring book in my lap, I could hear their conversation:

"You had a good day, Miriam?"

"Yeah. The same as usual. Made the beds. Cleaned the house. Shopped a little on the Avenue. Cooked. Nothing different." A pause. "And you, Moish?" she asked, calling him by his Yiddish name.

"I made my deliveries. Today I was in Queens. No new orders. Business is a little slow."

"Slow?" she'd ask softly.

"But it always picks up. You don't got to worry. I always pay the bills."

"I don't worry about the bills," she'd state firmly, her voice rising a bit.

"Good, because those worries you don't need."

Then, the conversation would stop, and the sound of silverware would fill an awkward silence.

"The mail?" Father would finally ask. "You got the mail, Miriam?"

"The mail can wait. First, digest your food. I got a good piece of fish and made the dessert you like, the graham crackers with the chocolate pudding in the middle. The mail can wait. We don't want no more ulcers from you getting upset from the bills."

"The mail, the bills, they're not what gives me ulcers," he'd correct her.

"Please, Moish," she'd plead, her voice lowered. "We don't need to talk about what gives you ulcers."

I didn't know what ulcers were, but I assumed they were something that shouldn't be talked about. Once again, I felt the tension in the air.

Father paused after her last remark, and then changed the subject: "The cantaloupe's sweet. You picked a good one."

"It doesn't take a genius. You touch one, smell it, and when it's ripe, you know it."

"Well, I'm still a lucky man. To start a meal with a sweet piece of melon is good."

She would place the rest of his dinner in front of him. "Digest. Eat slowly." She remained at the sink cleaning up and joined him at the end of his meal when they each had a glass of tea with a cookie. I would wait to hear him suck his tea through the sugar cubes he'd placed in his mouth, and hearing no discord, I walked to my room, giving myself permission to sleep.

CHAPTER 2
ROOM BY ROOM

As the youngest child on our block, I was the only one not yet in school. I spent my days at home with Mother, following her from room to room. If she was looking for something in her room or sitting on her bed sorting laundry, I brought in my doll and played there. She never let me help her. "You'll have all your life, plenty of time to do such things later. Now, just watch your mama and learn."

I sat on the worn cushion of her oversized armchair, moving about restlessly. My legs weren't yet long enough for my feet to touch the floor, but it was from that chair that I kept her company, peering into the private places of her room.

The furniture in Mother and Father's room spoke of another culture and another time, which I became familiar with through Mother's stories. I saw hints of it in the dark complexity of the carved headboard of their double bed and matching bureaus, each drawer intricately shaped, every handle ornate. When the bed was made and the furniture drawers were shut, everything looked immaculate. Yet the inside of Mother's dresser was forever disorganized. Crammed into every corner were panties, bras, cardigans, and dozens of anniversary cards.

I never understood why she bothered to save them, since each one looked the same: standard greeting cards, reading "To My Beloved Wife" on the outside, with token sentiments inside. I never heard such loving words expressed between my parents and wondered why Father wrote them in the cards. I noticed, too, that only one or two were signed, "Your loving husband, Morris." Most of them were formal and impersonal, signed, "Your husband, Morris."

Although Mother told me she took great care to select her cards for Father, I admired him for his sense of order when he tossed them out. I also marveled at the meticulous manner in which he kept his chest of drawers: socks rolled up and color-coded, underwear folded, the washed and pressed shirts picked up from Mr. Davis's laundry neatly stacked.

I adored looking at their wedding pictures. In one photo, I could almost feel the smooth satin and lace of Mother's full-length gown, which she told me she rented and returned the very night of their wedding. "Everything except my panties, my stockings, and my brassiere was rented: the gown, my veil, the necklace, my shoes, your father's tuxedo, white fancy shirt with the stiff collar, even the white bow tie. We rented everything from a store on Pitkin Avenue."

I couldn't imagine anyone else looking so pretty. The lace veil that framed her face gracefully caressed the length of her gown and flowed gently to the floor. She looked down at the teardrop bouquet of white lilies she held, so I could only see her long eye-lashes; her eyes remained hidden.

It wasn't until I was about nine that I found the courage to ask: "Were you excited the day you got married? Brides I see in the movies always look so happy. I can't tell if you were happy or not."

To my surprise, she said, "You're a smart girl. You're right, mamaleh. You see a lot," she said, looking at the photograph. "No, I wasn't very happy. Not one of my sisters, none of us girls was happy on our wedding day. You should never know from getting married without a mother and father to be with you."

Sighing, she concluded, "Why think about that now? What's the use talking? You don't need to hear about such things!"

I was always struck by what a handsome couple they were, more like movie stars than the parents I knew. When I looked at the tiny white lily-of-the-valley boutonniere pinned to Father's tuxedo jacket, I knew Mother must have ordered it to match her bouquet. She always knew about what Father called "style."

I looked at the photo so often and so intently, I felt as if I had been at their wedding. Mother insisted I wasn't. Sometimes I didn't know what was real and what was not.

On the days when Mother would take me out of the house to go shopping on Brighton Beach Avenue—or "the Avenue," as we all referred to it—Brighton bustled with energy. Mother and I would pass the grocery store, fish store, butcher shop, and fruit and veg-etable stand. Vendors displayed their colorful stock, knowing that

11

the moment a salesperson's back was turned the women shoppers would touch, pinch, and squeeze before selecting the best lettuce, tomato, or melon.

"Next time, a little gentler please," storekeepers would say, turning around, hands on hips. "Someone else, please God, will be eating that after you've squeezed it and thrown it down. You wouldn't want I should let someone to touch what you'll be eating, would you?"

Chickens hung from hooks inside the poultry markets, where each was cut and salted in front of every customer, as kosher tradition dictated. We browsed Aufrichtig's Appetizing Store with its abundant supply of exotic cheeses, herrings, lox, whitefish, and tuna salads. Snatches of dialogue in Russian, Polish, Hungarian, and Yiddish hung in the air.

The old country surrounded us as we walked past delicatessens luring us in with window displays of salamis hanging above trays of sizzling hot dogs on a grill, the sauerkraut nearby, pastrami and corned beef steaming in their bins fogging the windows. Such delis, open from early morning until after midnight, were common meeting places where people ordered a glass of tea, knowing they would be given a free basket of bread. Those who could afford an occasional meal out did so on Sunday, the busiest day of the week for all restaurants in Brighton.

Subways whistled and roared, but only visitors to the Beach heard them. For those of us who lived there, it was the background noise that lulled us to sleep. The sun and the salt air promised carefree summer days outside with friends.

In summers, we turned Mother and Father's bed around, placed it between the two windows, and then opened the living room door, which the bed had leaned against during the winter. "This is for cross-ventilation," Mother explained. "Now the air will have somewhere to move. At least we will be able to breathe."

We re-hung their sepia-toned wedding photograph above their bed. Two ornately framed photos of Mother as a bride remained on either end of her dresser. A mirrored tray with gold leaf edging lay between them, holding bottles of toilet water she proudly referred to as perfume.

Mother was in control during those times, telling Herbie and Father where to move the bed, how not to scratch the floor, and instructing them about the right way to roll up the forest green carpet. They followed her commands. I was allowed to carry one pillow, sometimes two. The carpet, warm to our feet in winter, was rolled and tied up, leaving the parquet floor bare and cool. It was one of the few predictable activities the four of us did together each year, and I always looked forward to this preparation for the hot days and nights of July and August. It was as though we were on holiday, vacationing.

I watched as Mother packed away the white linen duvet covers and winter quilts, protecting them from the moths of summer. She lovingly cradled them in her arms, placing them neatly into the cedar chest at the foot of the bed. Each duvet had scalloped edges with embroidered circular openings at its center. The checkered borders of the quilt remained hidden from view, safety-pinned in each of the duvet's four corners. Mother said: "This way they'll be covered neatly, keep their shape. I pin them, mamaleh, to prevent them from balling up inside."

Each time she said that, I couldn't help but think that was how I felt, hidden from view so that whatever was all balled up inside me was never seen.

At summer's end, when September rolled into October and November, darkness came early. Mother stuffed rags—torn nylon stockings, old cut-up undershirts and underwear—around each of the windowsills. "This is what I must do to stop the drafts from coming in. If we had a human being for a landlord and not an animal, a person with a heart who took care and gave us storm windows, this I wouldn't have to do. But we need protection, mamaleh."

When I was five, she still bathed me in the kitchen sink on Friday afternoons before sundown. Every week she told me, "See? The oven is on so my mamaleh won't catch pneumonia."

She still cradled me in her arms, gently placing me in the warm water inside our white porcelain kitchen sink, scrubbing me clean before wrapping me in a heavy towel and bundling me in flannel pajamas.

Then she bathed me in the bathtub until I was ten and later allowed me to take a shower, running the water until it was steaming. To avoid using too much hot water, she showered with me, even helping me to wash my body and my hair. I would have preferred privacy, but I also felt her love.

Since everyone referred to me as "Herbie's sister Linda," that's how I thought of myself, too. It's also how I believed God knew me. So when Mother lay next to me in bed as I said my nightly prayers, I said, "God bless Mother, Father, brother Herbie, sister Linda, our whole family, and the entire world."

Though I welcomed Mother's warm body next to mine, a part of me felt I was too old to need her so close by. Yet it was an indication that our world was at peace, because she was at peace. During those times, I could allow myself to drift off to sleep, as I heard Mother say: "You're a good girl, mamaleh. Sweet dreams."

CHAPTER 3
LEFT BEHIND

Mother, named Mariasha at birth, was born in 1908, the fifth of eight children, in the tiny village of Tolochin, near the town of Orsha, southwest of the city of Moscow. Her parents' marriage was an arranged one. Her father, Chaim, came from a long line of butchers and was the co-owner of a kosher butcher shop. Her mother, Ruchel, was the second of sixteen children, eight of whom died in childbirth.

Ruchel was beautiful and resourceful. In her teens she had worked for relatives in the city of Odessa and developed a love for city life and the culture it offered. She later shared stories with her children of all that she had seen and yearned for them to experience.

With the money she earned in Odessa, Ruchel helped each of her siblings to gain an education. Ultimately, each one achieved a professional degree: one became a dentist, another a lawyer, another an executive with a branch of Singer Sewing Machines in Moscow, and a few became teachers. One sister, who today might be described as Bohemian, took off for South Africa to design hats and women's clothing. For Jewish people—women, in particular—that was a rarity in Russia at the turn of the twentieth century.

Mother's parents were devoted to their children and shared the dream of a better life in America. Whenever Mother spoke of her father, Chaim, I'd watch her eyes light up in a way that they never did when speaking of anyone else. Undoubtedly, that was because her only memories of him were childhood ones. When he returned home each evening, she ran out of their thatched-roof house down the dirt path to greet him. He would scoop her up into his arms, lovingly pinch her cheeks, and tell her, "You are my little angel girl, my beautiful Mariasha, beautiful just like your Mama."

In 1913, Chaim—along with many Jewish men at the time—decided to leave his family and earn enough money in America to set up a proper home. He intended to send for everyone within the year. Mother was not yet five, and her mother was thirty-four, pregnant with her eighth child.

Mother's three older siblings were told about their parents' plans, but the day her father left at dawn, he did not wake the younger children to say goodbye. "It will be easier to leave without seeing them, without facing their tears," he told his wife.

His disappearance that night was a shock from which Mother later said she never recovered. "No one should know what it's like to have one day a father, a loving father who hugs you and holds you, and then you wake up one morning expecting to see him, and there's no more father. Can you imagine? What can be more terrible for a little girl who worships her tateh? No tateh. No hugs. No tea. No goodbye."

Four months after his furtive immigration to America and after his eighth child, a son, Abrasha, was born, Chaim sent money saved from working two jobs to pay for the baby's *bris*. A few months later, Chaim sent additional money along with steamship tickets for the entire family to join him in Wilkes-Barre, Pennsylvania.

Although still recovering from a difficult childbirth, Ruchel excitedly sold all the family's furniture and began to pack the clothing, bedding, and memorabilia she didn't wish to leave behind. It was 1914, the start of World War I. Three days before they planned to leave, the borders were closed.

Ruchel had to abandon her empty house in Tolochin and move into her parents' house, which was hardly large enough for the elderly couple. Now it had to be home to Ruchel and her eight children. Such an arrangement might have been tolerable for a night or two, but as the days and nights multiplied, along with the uncertainty of war, the family's distress mounted.

Herbie and I heard many stories about how Mother and her sisters and brothers managed to survive the war years. Even though the older children had been studying in a Talmud Torah, a Jewish school where they learned Hebrew in the morning and Russian in the afternoon, now they had to work with their mother to ensure their survival. The younger children—Mother included—only attended school when the schools were open and when they had clothing and shoes that fit them.

Desperate to keep her family together, Ruchel quickly developed the skill of a shrewd businesswoman, managing a kiosk at the Orsha railroad station where trainloads of soldiers stopped to buy food. She learned to avert her eyes from the lonely and often raucous soldiers, and she protected her beautiful older daughters by dressing them in boys' clothing.

Weeks sometimes passed, Mother told us, before she and her younger siblings would get to see their mother. For those visits, Ruchel woke at four or five in the morning to begin the miles-long trek to the kiosk. Once there, they would heat water for tea and cook food in time for the soldiers to buy breakfast. They'd remain there all day, and often—when it was too late to return home—they would have to sleep in a tiny back room of an uncle's house near the station.

The younger children suffered, as they longed for their mother's presence. As the war escalated, they were forced to stay at home with their elderly grandparents, who lacked the patience and energy to care for them. When there wasn't enough bread or potatoes to go around, they were sent to live in government-run institutions. They were grateful for the food and warmth, but as Jewish children, they were ostracized. "Where are your horns?" one boy asked Mariasha. "Why did you kill our God?" another asked one of her sisters. The girls were at a loss to understand such accusations.

When an epidemic of scarlet fever broke out, their friends—neighborhood children they had known since birth—began to die. Three of Mother's siblings, Gilka, Leah, and Abrasha, survived only because Ruchel stayed with them when they were quarantined in an open field miles from home.

An ocean away, my grandfather, Chaim, who had expected to see his family within a year, now spent nine years without them. His life in America turned out to be, in its own way, almost as tortuous as his family's life in Russia. He did not see his oldest daughter, Fanya, grow into a young woman of nearly twenty. And he had never seen Abrasha, the son who was born after Chaim left for America.

Yet Chaim continued to work hard in the hope of being with them again. He became a co-owner of a kosher butcher shop and general store in Wilkes-Barre, where he was active in an Orthodox synagogue. In 1920, two years after the war ended, he finally was able to contact his family, and with the help of influential members within his Jewish community, he sent the proper papers and secured tickets for them to immigrate to America in 1922.

In a letter, he proudly wrote: *My dearest wife and children: Now, at last we will be together again. You will travel to America with Second Class tickets, not like me when I came over in Steerage. You will have a good journey in the ocean that will bring you here, and the people from my shul and all the Jewish people from this town will be here to greet you. Your loving husband and father, Chaim.*

In the exciting weeks of preparation that followed, Ruchel relied on Mariasha, whose rosy-cheeked health and compliant nature meant she would be called on to do chores the others refused. As Mother remembered it all, Ruchel would say: "You must help your Mama. Oh, my child, we have so much to do now. The older children are out working, and I must turn to you. You are healthy and you understand what your mama needs."

When my mother once dared to ask why she was the one who always had to help, she was told not to ask why. So she said nothing more. She assumed she did not have a choice, so she did whatever had to be done, swallowing whatever resentment she may have felt. She was a good girl.

Later, Mother claimed that when the freedom to say "no" was taken from her, she became forever fearful to question anyone in authority, to disagree, or to speak for herself.

There was one story, in particular, that Mother told and retold to me and to my brother. Each time she began, we knew it was a bad sign.

"Just as we were readying to go to America," she would say, "my mama began to hemorrhage and was taken to the hospital. I was only twelve. I visited her each day during lunchtime. The hospital was on the same grounds as my school, and I crept through an opening in the fence to get to the front door."

One day, little Mariasha walked to the hospital in shoes too small, too tight for her feet and soles too thin, and climbed the stairs to her mother's room. The first person she saw was a sixteen-year-old Gentile boy mopping the hospital corridor.

She had seen the boy before. Whenever Mariasha brought her mother a kosher meal, the boy would scoff: "What's the matter?" he'd said. "Our food isn't good enough for you? You think you're better than we are? Well, you're not. I don't know why we even bother to take care of your mother."

My mother never knew the boy's name, but the sight of him that day made her tremble. It was clear that he was waiting for her. When he saw her approaching, the boy looked away for a moment, and then looked at Mariasha and announced in a mocking voice, "Your Jewish animal is dead!"

Mariasha turned toward her mother's room, her heart pounding in her chest, but was stopped by a nurse who reprimanded her: "You can't go in there today. Go back to school. When you go home, tell your family to make arrangements for the body to be taken away."

The body taken away? Images surfaced, reminders of the many moments she'd spent with her beautiful mama. She remembered how her mother brushed her hair lovingly, making her feel beautiful and special with each stroke.

More thoughts raced through Mariasha's head. What if she had gotten to the hospital sooner? Would her mother still be alive? The thought was more than Mariasha could bear. She couldn't have known that because the war had only recently ended, doctors and medical supplies were scarce. Patients were being operated on without sterilized instruments, and her mother's weakened body could not survive such abuse.

As Mariasha ran out of the hospital and followed the dirt road leading into the forest toward home, her confusion turned to panic. She felt abandoned in a world riddled with danger. With images of her mother in her head and echoes of the words "animal" and "body" in her ears, she cried out, "Mama, Mama!" She failed to notice that the frozen pond she'd crossed in the morning had since thawed. Mariasha fell onto a patch of thin ice, bruised and scraped her knees, soaked and ripped her dress.

Frantically, she picked up handfuls of snow and tried washing the blood away. When she finally reached home, her grandmother confronted her: "Look what you did to yourself! We don't need a tomboy in this family."

Sobs she had held down rose from her chest, and she cried uncontrollably: "Mother's dead. She's dead." She gasped for breath. "They told me she's dead!"

Only weeks later, Mother and her siblings learned that their father—after finally arranging for his family to be reunited—had died of pneumonia. Antibiotics had not yet been discovered, and he died in America never knowing of his wife's death in Russia.

The children were warned by relatives not to inform the government that they knew of their father's death. They would not have been permitted to leave without having a father to sponsor them.

Months later, they arrived on Ellis Island—my mother, her brothers, and sisters—each an orphan, each at the mercy of distant relatives, none of whom could afford to care for them, and some who openly admitted not wanting them. For the rest of her life, Mother refused to visit new places. Part of her remained forever trapped on that icy pond, frozen with fear.

Mother's family in Russia, L - R: Mariasha, Polya, Ruchel, Isaak, Chaim, Leah (on lap), Fanya, Basya

Father, Morris Appleman's passport photo, 1920

*Mother, summer before
her wedding, 1932*

Portrait of Mother as a bride

Wedding photo, Miriam & Morris Appleman, 1932

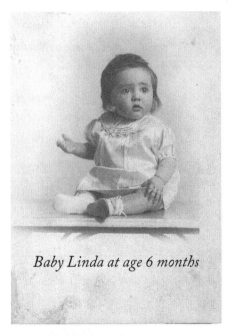

Baby Linda at age 6 months

Mother, baby Linda, Herbie, Father,
Summer 1942

Linda, age 2, in alleyway of
Brighton Beach home

Linda & Herbie, circa 1945

CHAPTER 4
THE DESCENT

I often wished Mother's stories were just tales, not a part of any-one's real life, least of all hers. "What's the use to look back?" she would say. Yet looking back was what she was compelled to do, especially when she was not herself. Her mind would transport her to where she was most determined not to go. In the telling, she was taken from us.

By day's end she'd be exhausted, and when I'd see her lie down on the sofa to watch our tiny television, I'd cling to the hope that the next day would be different. It never was. I lay awake listening to her pace through our rooms all night, mumbling incoherently, and I was unable to let myself fall asleep. When I did, nightmares followed, and I couldn't distinguish between what was real and what was not.

By morning, Mother couldn't make eye contact with any of us. She would mumble something, but it was only to God or some-times to the dead. Once again, I knew she was lost to me. Some-how, both still and restless, one moment she'd be ranting, and the next she'd be curled up in a corner of the room. My body would tense with every shift in her mood.

As long as she could show Father that she was able to straighten up the house and have dinner on the table when he returned home, he'd hold out hope and, I suppose, pray that "it" would pass. Yet when her sleepless nights were no longer random but occurred nightly, we all knew what would follow.

During the day, she would compulsively wash both the kitchen and bathroom floors, down on her hands and knees, re-washing and re-waxing sections made spotless moments earlier. With the scrub brush held tightly in her hands, her knuckles bone-white from the pressure, she would rock and scrub, scrub and rock, her energy and strength both frightening and hypnotic.

I was left alone with her until even Father could no longer remain in denial. Raving continuously in rapid, staccato whispers or loud, disjointed speech, she'd cry out: "What's to see? What's to remember? One day there's a family, a house, vegetables in the garden, a sun that shines. Then, boom! There's no more sun. No more tateh, no father. No hug. No goodbye. Gone to America. Mama tells us we'll join him soon. But, no, that never happens. The midwife comes. The baby is born."

Mother would lift her head to look across the room, her sad eyes squinting, focusing on a place far beyond Brighton Beach, Brooklyn. "We have the *bris*," she'd report. "Weeks later, Mama's not well. She tells us tateh is ready for us to come to America. Every one of us is hopeful. All the furniture is sold. Then, what do you think? War. We can't leave Russia."

As she dusted every piece of furniture or mopped the floor,

she'd talk about the war as though she were living it all over again. I felt I was experiencing it with her. She rinsed the mop, strangling it with a twist of her wrists. "What can Mama do? What can we all do? There is no choice."

When the dark days worsened, Mother would pull off all the bed linens, crumple them up, and then haphazardly throw them into the laundry bin before changing beds she'd already changed the day before. "You can't change nothing," she'd sigh. "So, what's the use? It doesn't matter anyways. Nothing matters."

I remained at her side, a silent witness, wondering where she was when her eyes lost focus. Was she recalling her father's departure for America, never saying goodbye? Was she remembering the terrible years of the war, the sacrifices made simply to survive? Was she mourning her parents who died just before they were all to be reunited?

Had she at least looked at me, I would have known that she was aware of my presence. I would have felt her love. Instead, all I experienced was her distance and transformation into an unpredictable, frightening creature, but one whom I could not let out of my sight.

In those years before I started kindergarten, when I stayed at home with her during the bad times, Herbie would take off for school and Father would go to work. Before leaving, Herbie always said, "See ya later, kiddo. Take care." Then he'd hesitate for a moment, as though about to say something more, but he never did. Maybe he, too, felt he was protecting me by never talking to me about our mother's illness.

Father would wash and dress, and then I'd hear him walking around the kitchen table. Yet, he never looked at me or explained anything when I entered the room. In a stern, sorrowful voice, he'd repeat his euphemism for Mother's condition: "Linda, your mama's not herself today."

Then he'd put on his jacket and ask Mother: "Will you be all right today, Miriam? Can I go to work? Tell me what to do."

"Go, go," she said. "It don't matter if you stay or if you go."

I secretly wished that he'd stay, but he never did. Instead, he'd kiss us both on the cheek and leave the house, never turning back to wave goodbye. Hunched over, looking shorter than his five feet seven inches, he'd leave me alone with my mother for the rest of the day.

I would crouch on the kitchen floor, in a corner against the side of the cold refrigerator door—the best lookout spot in the room. Silently, tucking my summer pinafore under my knees, I watched as she washed the floor and then re-washed the dishes, moving aimlessly through our rooms.

When it was time for Father to come home, she'd rush to put something together for dinner. She never ate with us during those times, but would serve us and then retreat to the sofa. This was one of the times when the worst could happen. Herbie somehow managed to eat, but then he'd leave. "I'm going to Larry's," he'd announce. "The guys are going to listen to the Yankee game." Acting as though everything was perfectly normal, he'd skip down the stairs and be gone.

As Friday approached each week, I would become increasingly fearful, anticipating her ritual preparations for the Sabbath and my bath, something she was determined to do after cooking and cleaning all day. In that state she handled me roughly, forgetting to test the hot water first. It was as if I'd become yet another object in the house in need of scrubbing.

After one such bath, I remember Father looking at me with a puzzled expression and saying, "Mamaleh, don't bite your nails. Mama gave you a nice bath? Yes?" I never answered.

The meal that followed was equally oppressive. Mother served us her homemade chicken noodle soup, baked chicken with Del Monte peas and carrots, and homemade applesauce for dessert. We ate in silence, dishes clanking loudly on the table.

One morning I woke to the sounds of Mother thrashing about and Father running after her. I sensed the fear behind his angry words. The tattered nightgown she wore day after day creased in upon itself between her breasts, filling the space where I pictured her heart pounding beneath its sheer fabric.

I wished that whatever was wrong with Mother was physical, as when she winced and massaged her lower back with her knuckles and said: "Oy, my poor back. The *bayner*, the *bayner!*" (The bones, the bones!) I understood an aching back, but Mother's wounds were invisible.

Father would yell at her. "Today, I can't let you stay at home. I'll take you and Linda to Esther's, where she will look after you, and I won't have to spend the whole day worrying. Is that asking too much? To just let me work?"

Mother burst out: "Sure! Sure! It's always about you. I need to make it easy for *you*. Well, I'm the sick one, and I want to stay here where I belong. Here in my house and not at Esther's. But that's asking too much."

I questioned only one time why Mother was saying she didn't want to go to Aunt Esther's. I even said that I didn't understand what was happening. Father leaned against the wall with his arm outstretched, as if to stop the wall from caving in. Then, staring at the floor, he replied angrily, "Everything's okay. Everything's fine. Just eat your breakfast."

I was not yet five, and Mother had always made me breakfast, served it to me, and kept me company while I ate. "To cook, *Lindichkeh*," she'd say, "you have all your life to do. Now, you have a mama who can make your food and sit with you while you eat."

I no longer had that mother. So I ate nothing and didn't tell Father.

Then, just when I thought he was about to tell me something important, something to help me understand, he said, "Go, get yourself dressed so I can take you and Mama to Aunt Esther's."

Mother would put on one of her old bras, one with thick shoulder straps to support what she called "my breasts that got stretched in Russia." Then she'd pull a housedress off a hanger, throw it over her undergarments, and roll a pair of nylon stockings down over her ankles, sighing as she bent to tie her shoes. Before leaving the house, and without even glancing at me, she would open each of the windows. "I must let the cold air from outside to come in and sweep through our rooms, mamaleh. The ocean breezes, they'll let me breathe." But the breath of air would last only a moment.

My father's brother Ruby and his wife, my Aunt Esther, lived half an hour away in the Brownsville section of Brooklyn. As soon as we arrived, my aunt would serve Mother and me breakfast. Later, she would give us lunch. I never understood why, but Mother always ate at Aunt Esther's, and she did whatever my aunt told her to do.

"Just rest, Miriam, dear. Lie down on the sofa, and I'll give you a nice blanket to cover yourself with," she'd say lovingly. "You know you always feel better when you rest."

Then Mother would lie down on the sofa, and Aunt Esther would cover her. I would sit nearby in a chair and fill in one of my connect-the-dots coloring books. Some days, Aunt Esther invited me into her kitchen to watch her roll out dough as she prepared to bake a challah or fancy cookies. It was good to be with someone who talked kindly and pinched my cheeks softly, like Mother did when she *was* herself.

Although Mother did nap, she would suddenly awaken from time to time, rambling the way people do in movies when they're talking in their sleep. "You can't change nothing, so what's the use of talking? Why think about it? It doesn't matter anyways. Nothing matters."

CHAPTER 5
LOST IN THE WARS

In 1945, the year I was to enter kindergarten, Harry Truman was president and World War II had recently ended. Everyone in Brighton had adored F.D.R., and Father, too, had been convinced that he was a good man.

Eleanor Roosevelt had found her voice as First Lady, and Mother often spoke of her admiration for her feistiness. Most women in Brighton enjoyed referring to the President's wife as "Eleanor," and talked as though she were a personal friend who fought for what was important to them: world peace and the rights of working women, mothers, and wives. "Such a brave soul. Imagine, a person so homely looking being able to speak her mind. It's remarkable," Mother said with envy.

"Sure, sure, if you had her education, you could speak out, too," Father responded.

"Oy, Moish, what's wrong with you? It's not just education. I have no confidence when it comes to talking. Not since my teacher in Russia embarrassed me by calling on me when I didn't even have my hand raised."

Father replied, "You know what the joke is? If she had your beauty, she probably wouldn't need her confidence. Anyways, she's a good woman. A good heart, and brains, too." He laughed and added: "I wouldn't want her in my bedroom, though!"

"Please! You're all alike, you men."

Until then, I had believed that Father agreed with Mother, who had taught me "never to judge a book by its cover." Now I heard, as she did, that he was more concerned with how women looked on the outside and was less appreciative of what was inside, which is what Mother valued most. I wondered if he felt that way about Mother, too.

Our entire neighborhood was home to immigrants who imbued it with the rich flavor and character of a *shtetel*, a small Jewish village in pre-war Eastern Europe. When I ventured outside, I saw the iceman deliver his ice—large blocks wrapped in canvas, strapped to his back—or heard the rag man sing from his horse-drawn wagon, "Rags for sale, rags for sale."

Mother sent me to a particular grocery store whenever she didn't have enough money. "Go, mamaleh," she'd say. "Go to The Refugees. Tell them your Mama is tired and will pay them for whatever you get the next time I see them." Then she told me the essentials we needed and reminded me to "ask for the *best* of everything."

I learned only years later that the grocers were not Mr. and Mrs. Refugee, as I had assumed. Everyone called them "The Refugees" because they had immigrated more recently than did my parents or my friends' parents.

When I entered their small, crowded store, I'd wait my turn before asking for a nice rye bread, a good quarter pound of butter, and an excellent half-pound of fresh pot cheese, just as Mother had instructed. One of the two brothers who owned the store would place the items neatly into a brown paper bag. After adding up the total, he counted aloud in Yiddish, licked the lead tip of his pencil, and then wrote the amount due on the outside of the bag. I marveled at how he, like my father, added numbers in his head by rolling his eyes upward and then down again, mysteriously arriving at a sum.

I was frightened by the other numbers, though, the ones I saw on the brothers' arms beneath their rolled-up shirtsleeves. I had to force myself not to look at those numbers because Mother had told me never to stare at their arms.

"It will only remind them of terrible things," she would say. "In America, thank God, you'll never know from such numbers. Here, the Hitler devils won't dare to come. But the Refugees? God alone knows what they went through."

I walked home feeling proud that I had shopped like a grown-up. Yet once Mother had put the notion of devils into my head, I began to wonder if even our cozy neighborhood was still safe. Despite the fact that everything seemed familiar—the freshness of the ocean's salty air, the bright store displays of fruits and vegetables, the overhead screech of the elevated train—my sense of safety began to crumble.

It didn't matter that Mother had told me that Hitler devils couldn't come to America. By then, I wasn't sure I believed everything she said.

❧

I didn't know that our neighborhood was essentially a ghetto. Of the more than fifty families on our street alone, there were two non-Jewish families plus Angelina, our Italian neighbor downstairs.

I certainly didn't know that most of the world wasn't Jewish, which explains why I was shocked to learn that the Roosevelts weren't. Their name sounded familiar. I knew many families whose last name was Rose, Rosen, Rosenberg. How different was Roosevelt? Yet even as I learned that most people in politics or in any position of real power weren't Jewish, I didn't question why, just as I didn't say anything when I heard people talking about our neighbor Gussie, who like Angelina rented rooms in the basement of our house, saying that she had lost a son in the war. Except for those who had lost relatives, everyone's spirits seemed high. Television hadn't yet entered our homes, and the atrocities that had occurred had been far away and out of sight.

In the summer, before the sun's heat became too oppressive, I would join Gussie in the alleyway of our house each morning. I'd sit next to her in a matching, multi-colored, child-sized beach chair she'd bought for me, feeling the souvenir of its woven pattern on the backs of my thighs. As I sat and watched her flying fingers, I became pleasantly hypnotized by the rapid click-clacking of her knitting needles.

No one else spent as much time with me or lavished me with as much attention. She bought me needles of my own and gave me her leftover skeins of yarn. I gratefully mimicked whatever she did, creating my own version of European knitting. Gussie would smile and nod. "You're doing fine, Lindichkeh, just fine."

In her basement apartment, she served me Postum in a tiny cup, with hot milk, "the way you like it." Then she would hand me a napkin along with a tiny teaspoon she'd bought for me in Woolworth's. "A little cookie, you want, too?" she asked.

Though she was always so kind to me, I never saw her with friends. I didn't even know if she had any. I never asked because I respected other people's secrets; my world held so many that for me it was the norm.

Once I learned about Gussie's lost son, though, I grew fearful of becoming separated from Mother, of losing her or of having her lose me when we were on the Avenue shopping. I begged my mother to hold my hand. "Don't let go," I told her. "Don't stop to talk to somebody and forget that I'm with you."

I was unable to account for my feelings, since nothing from the outside looked any different. The loud whistling of the elevated trains hadn't changed, and the same delivery trucks drove by. The bustling world of Brighton was as crowded as ever, pulsating with life and activity. Yet my insides felt unbalanced, and I didn't know why. What I did know was that I needed to hold onto Mother tightly and stay right by her side whenever I could.

From overhearing grown-up conversations and news bulletins, I knew that war was on everyone's minds—and it seemed to be dangerous. Yet I couldn't comprehend what the world's war was or how children got lost in it. It seemed as shrouded as the mystery of my mother's illness. As a young child, I was trying to cope with anxieties about a world war abroad and a private war at home.

CHAPTER 6
NEW WORLDS

The morning after Labor Day, 1945, I stood with the other children who were waiting to enter kindergarten on the first day of school. Filled with excitement, we huddled together, our hands and faces scrubbed, our new school clothes washed and pressed.

Parents—mostly mothers—held our hands until a loud bell rang inside Public School 253. A lady with gray hair then stood at the top of the school's steps and announced: "Say your goodbyes now, please. Bring your name tags, walk up the stairs, and wait in the lobby."

With a nervous smile, Mother gave me a big hug, saying, "Be a good girl, mamaleh. I'll pick you up later."

Although I had recently become fearful of leaving her side, on this day I was too excited about going to school to feel frightened. As we entered the lobby, though, I noticed a girl cowering in a corner, tears rolling down her face. I only knew her from the neighborhood park, but still, I felt sorry for her. She had thrown up all over her dress and on her shiny Mary Jane shoes. The boys looked at her with disgust. Most of the girls turned their heads away so as not to stare.

I couldn't let myself think of her for too long. This was my entrance into the outside world. I was now in the same building where Herbie and the older kids from our street spent their days. Now, I was a part of it all.

In the auditorium, the smell of fresh paint filled the air. Dark wooden floors were freshly waxed. Heavy, ruby-red velvet drapes hung above huge windows on both sides of the room, and the curtains hanging across the stage were the same dark velvet, each side tied by gold braided tassels.

A pretty, young teacher wearing a red-and-white, checkered dress and matching red, high-heeled shoes instructed us to find our seats when she called our names.

"Linda Appleman, since your last name begins with the letter A, please sit in the first row, on the aisle seat." Later I was delighted to find myself seated next to Suzie, a girl I had recently met at the kosher butcher shop. We had watched the man behind the counter pluck two chickens clean, hack them up, wash, and wrap them for our mothers to take home. As we now sat next to each other, Suzie and I squeezed hands, watching a new world open to us.

I thought about Mother throughout the school day, but I made myself believe that she was busy and safe, because I didn't really miss being at home. I looked forward to the routine of each day in kindergarten: playing in the dollhouse, finger painting, having milk and cookies, enjoying rest period on soft mats, and story-telling time.

When I colored in my coloring books at home, Mother would say, "Good, mamaleh. It looks so neat and pretty the way you stay inside the lines like that." In school, though, I was told to splash different paints onto shiny white paper and mix the colors, creating whatever shapes gave me pleasure. Although Mother wouldn't approve of me getting my hands dirty, my teacher, Mrs. Firestone, told us to have fun with the colors, to enjoy how it felt as we swirled them around. Soon, painting became my favorite activity. There were no lines to hold me in, and no one to please but myself.

Afterward, I sat on my floor mat and listened to Mrs. Firestone read my favorite story, "Cinderella." Each time, I waited eagerly for the prince to choose Cinderella and for the book to end "happily ever after." A part of my brain was waking up to the wonders of fantasy. Spending the day in school gave me the freedom that Father probably felt at work, where he didn't have to worry all day.

Not until my walk home did I begin to feel nervous again. I would prepare myself for Mother's mood, whatever it might be, and hope it would be "normal" for the afternoon and evening. However, life at home continued to be uncertain. As always, we watched for changes in her behavior, the sleepless nights, the restless days. Even when we were together, each of us felt alone.

Still, despite her dark days, Mother wanted me to live what most families in Brighton thought must be the American Dream for young girls. She assured me that I shouldn't worry about the five dollars a week that she spent on piano lessons, which I begged for at the end of first grade. She said that squirreling away the pennies and dimes to pay for such lessons was something she'd be good at doing.

Ballet classes started and ended with standing at the barre, feet placed in first, second, third, fourth, and fifth positions, over and over again, before any of us was permitted to pirouette across a cold, splinter-filled floor. The only part of the hour I really enjoyed was hearing the French words identifying each movement. I sang them in my head: *Changement, Pirouette, Glissade.* Those exotic sounds brought me—if only for a few moments—to a place where I pirouetted not because I was forced to by the tapping of a teacher's cane at my toes, but because I was learning to free my body. The other girls seemed happy to be in class, but I felt silly crooking my arm and acting out the words to "I'm a little teapot short and stout; here is my handle, here is my spout."

When Mother was well, she met me after school with cold milk in a mayonnaise jar she had saved, along with cookies she'd wrapped in wax paper. For me, walking to the dance studio with her and seeing her joy as she sat outside the door, peering inside, was better than any of the lessons. She'd smile and wave from the doorway once class began, a look of pride on her face for being able to give her daughter an opportunity she never had. I struggled through the classes only because they made Mother happy.

When Mother wasn't up to it, she had one of the other mothers take me. On such days, without her presence or her smile, whatever sense of joy I usually felt was gone.

At school, everyone loved Mrs. Kellert, my first and second grade teacher, who made each of us feel special. With a warm smile and gentle touch on my shoulder, she'd say, "Good morning, Linda," pronouncing my name sweetly. Every time I learned a new word or printed another letter of the alphabet for the first time, Mrs. Kellert squealed with delight. I thought of her, I suppose, in the same way that Mother thought of the beach and the ocean; she was better than medicine. Each day she gave me hope and offered me a new way of seeing myself.

Knowing that she wouldn't be my teacher in third grade, a wave of uneasiness came over me on the last day of second grade before summer recess. The thought of not having Mrs. Kellert's positive presence in my life filled me with a sense of deep loss. I asked to get my sweater and hid in the closet in the back of our room, muffling tiny sobs I couldn't control. When I stopped crying, I remembered something I hadn't thought about since the night Mother returned home from a parent conference earlier in the year. Smiling, she had told Father and me that Mrs. Kellert described me as being "too serious for a little girl." I was sure my teacher had confused me with another student, especially when Mother added that she said, "She looks as though she carries the burdens of the world on her shoulders."

Why would Mrs. Kellert say such a thing about me? I often giggled with my friends in class. I always smiled, like everyone else, when she said hello to me. Most of all, I never understood why Mother repeated Mrs. Kellert's words with such pride, as though she thought they were a compliment. I didn't think so. Since I never wanted my teacher to believe I did anything wrong, I was very unhappy.

Luckily, Mrs. Kellert didn't ask why I had taken so long to get my sweater. When I came out of the closet, she smiled and touched my shoulder, saying: "Make sure to enjoy your summer, Linda. Have lots of fun! Lots and lots of fun." She didn't say that to everyone, and that did make me feel special.

All I could reply was, "Thank you." I didn't wish her a good summer, which I had really wanted to do. I was too filled with sadness and that familiar dread of not knowing what might be lying ahead.

CHAPTER 7
FIREWORKS

The air hung heavy from the day's heat and humidity, and the sky's pale blue still held lingering shades and shapes of pink in it. Right after dinner, we joined the crowds crossing Brighton Beach Avenue. We walked beneath the elevated train tracks, then down another block to the stairs leading up to the boardwalk. A block beyond the El, we could hear the surf, a reminder of the Atlantic Ocean's endless horizon, with the brush of its waves against the sand hinting at a constancy in the world, a dependability I could trust.

The moment the Fourth of July fireworks began, we broke into choruses of "oohs" and "ahs" that followed each new pattern that flashed across the sky, visible from our end of the boardwalk in Brighton to the other end in Coney Island. The grown-ups, too, were like children. The spirit of the night was contagious; the world seemed wondrous, filled with color and all sorts of possibilities.

The splendor of the night's stars couldn't compete with the man-made magic of the fireworks, which made the sky seem a painted canvas.

I awakened the following morning to the gentle warmth of early summer, still feeling the glow and thrill from the night before. Moments later, I was startled when my father suddenly entered my bedroom.

"Get up, Linda," he said, his voice tense. "Mama needs to go for a treatment today. Find a friend to come along for the ride."

I was eight years old. I didn't know what treatment Mother received. I only knew that when she wasn't feeling well, that's what Father said she needed. I assumed, in fact, that all mothers got "a treatment" when they needed to feel better.

I felt certain I could count on my good friend Anita. She wouldn't ask questions that I wouldn't be able to answer. As Mother would say, "She knew how to mind her own business." And a couple of days earlier, Anita had shared a secret with me.

Although everyone on the block knew that Anita didn't have a mother, no one ever talked to her about it. But that summer day, she interrupted our game of stoop ball. Her voice was calm, but her deep-set brown eyes filled with tears.

"You know, I have a Mama, too," she said. "Only mine's in heaven, and that's why you can't see her. I have a picture of her, though, and she's really pretty. I keep it under my pillow. Every night I pray for my Mama."

As Anita explained that her mother had died while giving birth to her, her tears became uncontrollable. "Sometimes I cry because I want her to come out of the picture and talk to me. She never does. My brothers say that's because she's in heaven and it's too far away for me to hear her. But they know she sees us and loves us, and they tell me I just have to keep praying for her soul to be in peace. I don't really know what a soul is, but I pray anyway because they tell me to."

It was then that I knew we were special friends, because she asked me to pray with her, saying, "I'm tired of praying alone." So, on the day when I needed a friend, I knew Anita would welcome company.

Since neither of our families had telephones yet, I had to walk to her house, crossing 2nd Street, then swinging left into her alleyway, Brighton 1st Court, a magical, miniature street, so narrow that cars weren't allowed to enter. Her house was the second of four on the left side of the court. Its garden, like ours, overflowed with weeds, more a patch of grass than a place for us to play.

I walked up the steps of her stoop and rang the bell to her upstairs apartment. When she opened the front door and saw me, she whispered apologetically, "My father's still asleep. He doesn't go to work until late in the afternoon." Her father drove a truck, delivering seltzer and soda bottles to people's homes.

I asked her if she could come with us for the ride to my mother's doctor. She gestured for me to follow her into the living room where her father was asleep on a sofa bed. She bent down and whispered in his ear.

With his eyes half-closed, he murmured hoarsely, "Yeah, yeah, sure. You can go with Linda." Then he quickly added, "Don't forget to be good!"

She kissed him on the cheek. "I'll be good, Daddy."

Back at our house, we saw Father pacing near the car. He shooed us into the back seat and then rushed upstairs to get

Mother. Moments later, he came out holding her by the arm, leading her down the front stairs. She was wearing a summer housedress, along with that frightened face I had seen flashes of in the days just before the Fourth of July. Father helped her into the car and locked her door. Once he began driving, neither of them spoke for a while.

Finally, Mother complained. "Again you're taking me! Again! What do you care about what they do to me? You who sit outside in the waiting room and never even talk to the doctor, never show no interest, no concern. You who call yourself a man!"

"Shhhhh…Miriam," he pleaded. "Please."

"Yeah, yeah," she continued. "Now I don't recognize people on the Avenue. People I know. One day I won't recognize my own children. What do you care? You don't get the treatments. You don't know nothing!"

They exchanged words in Yiddish and Russian, and soon their voices rose. Anita and I tried to talk over them. When they fell silent again, we filled the space by inventing word games, singing songs, or talking about our other friends.

Eventually, my father parked the car on a street with a row of brownstone houses, all facing Prospect Park. He told us, "Just wait in the car. Don't go anywheres, no matter how long we take."

I watched my mother and father walk the half block toward the doctor's office. When my father rang a bell, someone came out to usher them inside.

Anita and I sat in the car, praying for her mother. I repeated after her: "May God keep her soul in peace and let her look down on us and send us her love because we want to know that she can see us and help us." It felt good to pray with my friend.

I wondered, though, whether it was also possible to pray for someone who wasn't dead.

In the trips to the doctor's office that followed, we brought along coloring books or school readers. Sometimes, we'd play a game we called "Pretend," using our dolls to act out stories about happy families in some faraway place.

Each time Mother returned to the car after one of her treatments, she'd be paler, quieter than when she had left. I'd search her face, looking for the mother I knew, but I couldn't find her in the dazed, disoriented person who wasn't even aware of my presence. Yet compared to Anita, I felt lucky.

After several weeks and many car rides to the doctor's office, Mother began to appear more like herself. She combed her hair and spoke in ways that I could understand. I sensed it when she started to eat and to cook good meals again, and I knew it when I no longer needed the bathroom light kept on all night.

The treatments continued until August, but Herbie made the time to go to the beach with me before leaving to play stickball each morning.

"Come on, kiddo," he'd say. "Let's run over to the boardwalk. I'll take a swim, and then I'll teach you the side stroke again."

He'd put his hand in mine, and we'd walk, skip, or run the block and a half from our house to Bay #5, where the vast stretch of beach from Coney Island to Brighton was not yet peopled, the sand still damp, not yet warmed by the morning's sun. Those were sweet times, peaceful moments away from home. Herbie swimming, me mainly watching. The two of us alone, together.

When Herbie brought me back to the house, I'd sit and knit with Gussie in the alleyway or stay upstairs with Mother. Around noon, I returned to Bay #5 with my friends. Following our parents' instructions, we'd place our beach blankets close to the boardwalk, "just to be safe." Then, before swimming, we'd sit close to the ocean, wait for the big waves to pass, and as the smaller ones rolled gently onto shore, we'd build castles and bury each other in the wet sand. Later, we'd eat lunch out of brown paper bags; some friends brought hard-boiled eggs and fruit, a couple of peaches or a bunch of grapes. I'd always bring cream cheese with lettuce on rye toast. I loved the crunchiness of the lettuce on the toast, and after a day of floating on the ocean's salty waves, food always tasted better than it ever did at home.

By mid-afternoon, we'd be hungry again and would buy potato knishes or ice cream bars from one of the teenaged boys who sold them on the beach. One was my big cousin Herbie Letterman, my Aunt Lil's oldest son. Dressed in stiffly pressed white pants and a white shirt with the sleeves rolled up, Cousin Herbie would chant, "Ice cream here! Buy your Good Humor ice cream here!" He handed out the pops from a heavy box filled with blocks of dry ice hanging at his side, held together by straps crisscrossed around his shoulders and waist. Under the hot sun, the ice cream began dripping and melting the second we licked it. He, too, was dripping from sweat, and I felt proud that he was my cousin and sorry that he had to work so hard and couldn't be having fun with his friends on the beach. But he never seemed to complain.

My friends and I would leave the beach late, returning home only when the hot air gave way to warm breezes and the sand cooled between our toes.

Throughout the day, there were enough distractions to hold back the images of Mother going to the doctor, Mother pacing the floor during the night, and Mother acting agitated in the morning. On good days, she'd be relaxed by late afternoon when I came home. Being with her then was easier than in the morning, when she refused to leave her bed.

Some days, I found myself wishing I could stay at the beach forever.

Although August arrived hotter than the other months of summer, rainy days were more frequent, the weather less predictable. Everyone agreed the days passed too quickly and the summer ended far too soon.

I was excited to return to school and wanted to believe that my new teacher, my new class, and my mother would all be okay, and that I wouldn't have to worry about being too serious. So, in September, dressed in my freshly pressed white blouse, pleated skirt, and new Mary Janes, I smiled at everyone. I concentrated on looking like a happy, grown-up third-grader, even though Mrs. Kellert's words lingered, hinting that something was wrong with me. I would have to figure out how to get from one day to the next without having anyone think I was too serious or *too* anything. All I wanted to be was like everyone else—normal, or, better yet, perfect.

CHAPTER 8
SUNDAY RITUALS

In the 1940s and early '50s we kids played outside, rarely visiting one another inside our apartments, so I had no way of knowing if other mothers behaved differently than mine. I seldom saw my friends with their mothers, and though I had many aunts—six on Mother's side, six on Father's—I usually saw them only on weekends or for special occasions.

What I did know was that Mother looked older than the other mothers on our street. I assumed it was because she spent so much energy washing, ironing, and scrubbing floors. Also, she wore the same clothes on the Avenue as when she was at home—a housedress, black Oxford lace-up shoes, and nylon stockings rolled down over her ankles. The other mothers wore modern, flowery frocks, nylon stockings, and high-heeled pumps, which made the other mothers look more American, more like the ladies I saw in magazines.

Mother dressed up only on Sundays when we visited relatives or on rare occasions when we ate out at one of Brighton's family restaurants. Other than the half-hour a day she'd spend reading the *New York Post*, she seldom did anything for herself, never asked a neighbor or anyone else to help her, and was always tired and always alone. It didn't seem to occur to her to play with me, but then, how could she have known how to play when she spent her childhood simply trying to survive?

I know my mother did her best with me. It was she who taught me about kindness and compassion. When Mother was growing up, her father would often bring home an indigent Jew on the Sabbath to share the ritual family meal. Her mother would welcome the stranger warmly, later explaining to the children: "This is how to perform a good deed, a true *mitzvah*. To make someone feel welcome, you must treat him with respect."

Whenever we saw people on the Avenue who were crippled or children who looked poor and disheveled, Mother would say to me: "Nobody should think that just because God doesn't give someone a pretty face or a lot of money or because he makes someone else a cripple, that such a person doesn't have feelings or isn't good. Such a person may turn out to be the nicest person you'll ever know."

That was the wisdom she shared with me when she was well. She bought me coloring books and crayons, handed them to me, and told me, "Here, mamaleh, color." Then she'd return to her housework. In 1952, when we bought our first television set, her message changed to, "Go, Lindichkeh, watch a nice program." Western action films and love stories were my favorites, but even if Mother was in the very next room ironing, I still yearned for her to be sitting next to me. When I asked her to, though, she'd smile sadly, implying that there was something important I didn't understand about adults.

60

I was used to hearing people say to her, "She's too close to you, Miriam. She holds on to your apron strings. It's not good." I thought I knew what they meant, but I stayed close to her because that's what I thought she wanted. Not letting go of Mother felt both natural and necessary. After all, I was there to make her happy.

The dark side of Mother's life, the secret side, separated my father, my brother, and me from one another as much as it bound us inextricably together. When I was young, I believed that expressing feelings, particularly sad feelings, was dangerous. I never wanted to feel tangled in a web of emotions. I'd witnessed how they led Mother into states of confusion and terror. Therefore, I decided to be logical, to think things through, and not get trapped in a whirlwind. I never wanted to do what I saw Mother do when she lost control.

Nor would I lose myself in housework just to give my life a semblance of order. I had already seen Mother enter states of despair in which she demanded perfection of herself. Our clothes would be the cleanest and the starchiest of any kids I knew. The smell and feel of those clean sheets she'd change every Friday are as easy for me to recall today as the shiny, waxed kitchen floor that, when dry, was covered with brown paper to keep it free of our footprints.

The Sundays when Mother dressed up, we usually visited with family. However, not all Sundays were pleasant—especially when Father wanted to visit his sister, Pauline, who had multiple sclerosis, or when Mother felt obligated to visit her elderly aunt, *Tanteh*, with whom she'd lived when she first came to America. Herbie stayed with friends, seldom joining us for those visits, and no one insisted that he come. Meanwhile, I'd sit alone in the back seat of the car feeling a familiar queasiness.

"This is what families do," Father reminded my mother and me. "We can't forget the *altichkehs* (the old ones) or those who aren't well."

Aunt Pauline lived with my Uncle Morris on the first floor of a two-family house in the Brownsville section of Brooklyn. Uncle Morris was my favorite uncle, and both Mother and Father referred to him as a saint.

"He could have left my sister when she got sick," Father always said, as Mother would turn her head away to stare out the window. "No man had to do what he did. After all, he sacrificed having children when he always wanted a big family. And look what happened."

Once inside their apartment, I watched as Uncle Morris changed the position of Aunt Pauline's head the moment she seemed uncomfortable. When she needed to go to the bathroom, he lifted her out of her large armchair in the living room and carried her out. When she was hungry, he held her chin in his hand, fed her, and kissed her affectionately for all to see.

When my aunt's speech began to lose its clarity, Uncle Morris acted as her interpreter. That was even more disturbing. "Linda Londy Loo," he'd say affectionately, "Aunt Pauley wants to know if you're enjoying school." But his smile was loving, his hugs gentle, and he definitely showed me more tenderness than Father ever did.

Whenever we left Uncle Morris and Aunt Pauline, Father would say: "God should only look after him. Such a life no one deserves. Such sadness! It's a good thing my mother didn't live to see this."

On the ride home, I'd feel sad for all of us.

Tanteh, my mother's aunt, then in her nineties, lived at the Hebrew Home for the Aged. To get to the room she shared with three other women, we'd walk through the halls holding our breath to avoid inhaling the smell of urine that permeated the building. Old people were everywhere—in the hallways, in wheelchairs, in their beds screaming, curled up in a fetal position—many looking as though they had already died.

Occasionally, Tanteh said nice things, like the day she talked about Herbie: "So, your Chaim is some big shot, huh? He did all the haftorah and torah readings at his Bar Mitzvah. And his voice, he sang like Al Jolson, they say. No?"

"Yeah, yeah," Father replied. "He's a good boy, a good boy, our Chaim is."

I knew that Father's pride in Herbie came not only from his academic achievements but from the fact that, as a son, he held the promise of our family's future. Father had no expectations for me, or at least none that he expressed. At best, he probably hoped I'd marry and have children. Anything more than that he never mentioned.

The fact that many people remarked that I bore a strong resemblance to Mother made Father uneasy. I sensed it from the look in his eyes. If I fell and cried after scraping my knees, my tears caused him to panic. When I brought home a report card from grammar school, he assumed that everyone got A's. Only Herbie's grades seemed to matter.

At ten, when I was selected from MacLevy's Dance Studio to appear on television, Mother and Herbie came to the studio to watch. Father said he'd find a storefront with a TV and watch it with one of his customers. In the end, though, he forgot. He'd been too busy, he said, when he came home that evening. Then he sat down and had dinner. I didn't feel unloved, just unimportant.

Throughout those early years, when I believed I was the gift Mother needed to help heal her sadness, I clung to her. Yet I never felt that my birth brought any real joy to Father, so I followed his lead and kept my distance.

The person I cared for most, in our entire family of twenty-three aunts and uncles and twenty-five first cousins, was my Aunt Lil, Mother's younger sister. She and her husband, Uncle Bernard, and my cousins Herbie, Hannah, Ronnie, and Allen, all lived in the public housing units known as "the Projects." Small groups of men, mostly black, congregated in the shadows of the dull brick buildings, smoking, idly passing the time. This was in the early 1950s and the stereotypes about "those people"—black men, in particular—made me wary of them.

I never got used to the odors or the noise in Aunt Lil's building. People shouted, babies cried, the sounds of radios and TVs echoed in the halls, and graffiti covered the pea-soup-green walls, cracked and peeling. Yet I still looked forward to visiting Aunt Lil.

She told us how she went from door to door persuading people to sign petitions to extend rent payments if someone's husband lost his job. She also helped get the city to organize free baby-sitting for women who had to support their families alone. Somehow, she found the time and energy to advocate for such causes, though in my parents' eyes, she was unable to help herself.

I noticed, as did Father and Mother, that her apartment seemed dreary, that the floors weren't scrubbed clean and shiny like ours, and that the dust on the furniture added to the must-iness throughout the apartment's seemingly airless rooms. And I saw that Aunt Lil's shoes were never polished, always needing new soles, and her dresses—many of which had been hand-me-downs from Mother—were seldom ironed, never looking as they had when Mother had worn them.

Yet while my parents worried that Lil didn't care about what was important, I saw her as free-spirited, connected to the outside world, able to be both committed and playful. At family weddings or Bar Mitzvahs, Aunt Lil took herself onto the dance floor, her Sunday shoes in no better shape than her everyday ones. With the palm of her left hand cupped behind her head, her left elbow held out dramatically, her right hand at her waist, her right shoulder forward and her elbow faced outward, she danced the Russian squat-kicking dance, the *kazatski*, with a real or imagined partner, holding onto the skirt of her dress, flaring it back and forth with each exuberant step. A girlish giggle bubbled from her throat as she made her way across the floor.

I never knew Mother to laugh, at least not with any real gusto. And I knew that my other aunts kept their apartments tidier, fed their families good meals, pressed their clothes and polished their shoes, and made themselves more available to our family in our times of need. Yet that never made me appreciate them more. They were all consumed with worry—caring about their apartments, their children, and their husbands. I saw them all in different shades of gray, while Aunt Lil was colorful.

I wasn't yet able to understand how deeply each of Mother's sisters and brothers had been affected by their childhoods, the war, and the loss of both parents before immigrating to America. Still, I often wished that Mother could have brightened up and shared some of Aunt Lil's sparkle with me, if only once in a while.

During the ride home, Mother would ask Father: "Did you remember to give her a little something?"

"How could I not? Today, I gave her a ten-dollar bill. She slipped it into her apron and whispered, 'Thank you,' so the kids wouldn't hear."

Staring out the window of our black Pontiac, Mother would sigh. "All she knows how to do is make babies, but then she has no routine to care for them. My other sisters are all so organized and clean. I don't know what happened to Lil. Do you think it's because she was the youngest of the girls when my mother died?"

I thought Mother was probably right. Aunt Lil may have been too young to remember a time when her life had any order. Perhaps that's why she spent so much of her time fighting for political causes, for underdogs. She may not have had all her facts straight, as Father was eager to point out, but I saw her as noble, someone who could see what others needed and was willing to fight for them.

CHAPTER 9
GOD COMES TO BRIGHTON

Whenever Mother wasn't herself, Father would shut the blinds to prevent people from seeing in. Unable to describe what was happening, I was prey to so many unspoken fears that I concluded life would be far safer if I had God on my side. Yet I refused to summon the God that Mother called upon when she was sick. I wanted no part of her "Dear-Heavenly-Father-Show-Me-The-Way" God, who was either a figment of her imagination or an ineffective version brought over from Russia, and of no help to her here in America.

There was a God, though, with whom I felt a connection when I was in Borough Park, Brooklyn, at my Uncle Harry's house. Whenever I was with my uncle's family, in what my parents referred to as their "religious home," I experienced a feeling of health and wholeness.

The summer I was eight, I set out on a mission. My goal was to gain the security I believed their special relationship with God offered. I was sure it would protect me from the condition that constantly threatened not only my mother, but also my father, Herbie, and me. It was a way to separate myself from Mother's illness while remaining loyal to the healthy part that I knew would want me to have God on my side.

While Father was the sixth of his parents' eight children, Uncle Harry was the second child and the oldest son. He was the first to immigrate to America, before World War I. In the 1920s, he married my Aunt Bina, and together, they raised a family in Kentucky, where they owned a general store. They were eventually responsible for bringing my father, all of their other siblings, and their parents over from the other side. By the time I was born in 1941, they had already moved to Borough Park and placed their four children in *yeshivas* (religious schools).

Meanwhile, Uncle Harry was on his way toward amassing a fortune in real estate. He was the only relative my parents referred to as "rich." I wasn't impressed by his wealth, though, since he owned a modest house with drab furnishings. He and Aunt Bina were Orthodox Jews and obviously felt it inappropriate to pay attention to anything material.

But Aunt Bina's presence was powerful. Taller than Mother, with broad shoulders and a solid, square body, she wore dark, loose-fitting dresses with flat-heeled, lace-up shoes. Her hair was pulled into a bun at her nape, and she always looked as though she'd had just enough time to brush it and push in as many bobby pins as needed to keep it in place. Wearing no make-up, she had a particular beauty, an intelligent knowingness I had never before encountered. She loved reading the Bible, leading rallies for the state of Israel, and observing the Sabbath in temple.

I didn't understand why Father—far more handsome and better dressed—wasn't as successful as Uncle Harry. When Father spoke of him, he said: "A man like that doesn't need fancy suits. His shirts aren't even pressed. But his mind—quick like fire. Someone else sees only an empty lot. Harry looks at an empty lot and sees gold."

When I was getting to know my aunt and uncle in the late '40s, all of their children were grown. I felt certain that their weeks were easier than mine, if only because they were predictable. The family attended their neighborhood temple every week with the same people to observe the Sabbath. That day, they went nowhere, did nothing but rest or read, and sat quietly at home together as a family. That was what I found myself attracted to and what I desperately wanted to experience. So I conjured a scheme to bring the God of Borough Park to Brighton.

At the end of summer, with Mother in one of her better moods, I appealed to her to speak to Father on my behalf. Later that day, I overheard her talking to him.

"You'll never believe what I have to tell you, Moish. Our little Linda, she wants to go to *cheder*. She wants to study in Hebrew School. She says if Herbie went, she should go, too. I thought maybe you'd be proud to have a little girl who wants to study with the Bar Mitzvah boys. She's quick, like you, not like me. What do you think?"

"Cheder? A girl in cheder?"

"Yeah, why not?"

"Well, let me think about it."

"What's there to think? Be grateful she wants to go."

"All right, all right, so I'll think about it."

The following Monday, at the end of the first day of third grade, Father met me in the schoolyard. With a twinkle in his eye, he said, "So, you want to study Hebrew? Well, let's go and see if they'll take you."

We walked down Brighton's 6th Street toward Neptune Avenue, to the Hebrew Alliance, the Orthodox temple that served our community. Father and I walked up a flight of rickety stairs and entered the office of its four-room schoolhouse. With a nervous laugh, his face turning red, Father approached Mrs. Levy, the teacher for Class Aleph.

"How do you do? I'm Mr. Appleman, Morris Appleman. And this here is my little Linda, who wants to study Hebrew. Can you take her?"

Mrs. Levy smiled and said, "Well…"

Father interrupted: "She's a good girl. Smart. Wants to learn. What do you think?" Before she could answer, he added, "I'll be happy to drive home any children who live nearby when I come to pick her up after class. And if it's dark already, and you, yourself, need a ride, well, it would be my pleasure to drive you home, too."

"Aren't you kind," Mrs. Levy said, smiling at both Father and me. "I'd be happy to have your daughter in my class, Mr. Appleman.

Your Linda will be our only *maydehleh*, the only little girl. But don't you worry. I'll take care of her like she's my own."

I learned the Hebrew alphabet the first few days of class, and could read and write the language within weeks. Since we mostly practiced reciting prayers, I understood very little, but learning the language offered a significant link to my father and to the men in his family. I enjoyed the melodies we were taught to chant, and I even believed that God was beginning to reveal himself to me through my own hand, as I wrote from right to left in the narrow lines of my thin, blue notebook.

A few months later, when I was able to chant the prayers accurately, I asked Father to go with me to services on Saturday mornings. Until then, Father went once a year for the traditional Yiskor service honoring the memory of his parents, but we attended Synagogue primarily on the high holidays, Rosh Hashanah and Yom Kippur. He seemed all too pleased to get up early and walk to the synagogue with me on Saturday mornings. Since I was still a child, I didn't have to sit separately with the women upstairs, but was allowed to sit next to him in the men's section of the temple.

Although he seldom spoke to me during the service, our swaying together to the chanting and praying in the synagogue offered the feeling of protection I was seeking from the shadowy world of Mother's illness. Occasionally, Father patted me on the shoulder and said, "It's nice, nice being in *shul* with my Little Linda." And when he didn't seem to mind me braiding the fringes of his prayer shawl as I sat close to him, I was more convinced than ever that he had the God of Borough Park within him.

During such quiet times, I was able to breathe with ease. It was the closest I ever came to feeling like a child, at peace with Father and with God.

CHAPTER 10
ALONE

When Herb began applying to college, our family was shaken. Mother questioned his need to move away from home just to go to school, and Father didn't know why Brooklyn College wasn't good enough for him. Since Herbie had never raised his voice to them about anything, I was alarmed by the battles that occurred at the kitchen table, in the living room, or behind the closed door of my parents' bedroom. With the three of them shouting, it felt as though everyone—not just Mother—was out of control.

Finally, the principal and the dean of Herb's high school cornered Father into submission, telling him that it would be selfish if he and Mother didn't allow their son to accept one of the scholarships being offered by Ivy League schools. Not knowing my parents' reasons for wanting Herb to stay home, they told Father that if Herb wanted, he could accept the scholarship he was offered to Stanford University, three thousand miles away. So they suggested Father would be wise to let him accept the scholarship to Harvard, which was less than a day's car ride. Father gave in, Herb accepted Harvard's offer, and, the world as I knew it changed forever.

The week before Herb left, I stood in the doorway to our room watching him pack a duffel bag. Mother had been washing and ironing all week to get him ready. As he placed a V-neck sweater neatly on top of folded khaki pants, he noticed me standing there and stopped. I'd been thinking about how the room would feel when his bed, two feet away from mine, would be empty and how different it would be to go to sleep without knowing he was reading, his flashlight on, not wanting to keep me awake. I'd been thinking of the silence without the music from his radio.

Sighing deeply, he said, "I'll finish this later. Let's go for a walk."

It was Indian summer, the first week in September. The days were still hot, with occasional cool breezes coming from the ocean. I grabbed my white cardigan sweater, knowing Mother would want me to have it with me "just in case." She was on the Avenue shopping, and Father was at work.

Herb and I climbed the steps leading from the street to the boardwalk, and then he motioned for me to join him on one of the empty benches facing the ocean. The late afternoon sun warmed our cheeks, and the ocean sparkled in the distance. He turned toward me and looked directly into my eyes, reminding me of Father when I couldn't tell whether he was angry or sad. I felt a quiver in my stomach.

"You're going to have a great year in fifth grade," he began, a serious expression on his face.

"You think so?"

"Sure! And I can't believe you're the only girl in that entire Hebrew school. I bet in a few years a lot of girls will follow in your footsteps. I'm proud of you, kiddo."

"Thanks," I said, wondering where the conversation was really going.

"I'll write to you often and tell you all about Harvard and college life." Then, pausing, he added, "You'd better answer my letters."

"Of course I will."

He paused again. "Listen, Linda Londy Lou, we have to agree, here and now, to make a secret pact. Promise me that you'll write and tell me whenever anything's wrong." He added, with an uncharacteristic tremor in his voice, "Whenever Mom gets sick."

"What do you mean?"

"You know, Lin. When she doesn't sleep at night. When you hear her talking and walking around from room to room. When she acts strange in the morning and Dad takes her to spend the day at Aunt Esther's." He paused, and then continued, "If that happens, you'll have to let me know. Okay?"

"But you'll be far away. You won't be able to do anything. Why would I let you know?" Tears were starting and I didn't know why.

"I can't explain it. You'll just have to," he said, looking away. "Somehow, I'll find a way to help. I just haven't figured out how yet."

Herb was talking about Mother's getting sick when I expected him to be telling me how much he was going to miss me, how sad he was to be leaving me behind. Instead he was talking about Mother, something he'd never done before. Not once. So, why then? Why, just before he was about to leave?

I was afraid to ask him to tell me more about Mother's sickness, but I was also too angry, too sad. I just sat there, quietly smiling, twirling my hair. After a moment, I did what I knew how to do. I focused on him and tried to calm him down, instead.

"Sure, Herb, I'll let you know," I said, knowing that I would never keep such a promise. Why would I? What could he do anyway? Harvard was a million miles away. I didn't understand why he'd even bothered to ask. I vowed never to tell him anything worrisome about anyone.

In the days before he left, I continued to keep my focus on whatever he was doing. Watching him pack, I felt his excitement. I took out my map of New England and traced with a red crayon the car trip we were about to take from Brighton Beach to Cambridge, Massachusetts.

With Herb's ravenous appetite for good books, good food, baseball, the radio, and movies, he brought whatever life there was into our family. I read the jackets of novels he took out of the library, books by Dickens, Dreiser, Emerson, Dostoevsky, and other famous writers. But with him away, there'd be no new books. There'd be nobody to walk with me to the corner to buy chocolate truffles before drinking an ice-cold glass of milk. With him gone, there'd be no one to take me to a neighborhood matinee movie or invite me to go bowling on days when Mother wasn't quite herself but was still at home.

With him gone, I'd be left alone with Mother and Father.

CHAPTER 11
MOTHER, ARE YOU HERE?

Mother had held herself together throughout Herb's senior year in high school and even into the start of his freshman year at college. At Harvard, she lined the drawers of his dresser and made his bed so that his dorm room looked clean and cozy.

Not long after we returned from our trip to Cambridge, though, things changed. The descent was gradual; either Mother had known that she was losing control and was trying hard to maintain balance, or it was as much of a surprise to her as it was to me. I was ten years old, in fifth grade, and I was home alone with her during a school holiday.

In mid-morning I told Mother I was going out to play. With no warning, she burst into a frightening rage. In a voice trembling with fury and terrifyingly unfamiliar, she screeched, "Going out? No! You're not! You're going nowhere!" I took a step back in shock, but she lunged wildly toward me, her eyes unblinking, her words like whips. "You can't go out! No, I won't let you out!"

That's when she grabbed me, clutching my arms, her strength alarming. We were at the top of the stairs as she pushed me to the floor and sat on me. Sitting heavily on my back, she forced my face and body onto the cold floor. Filled with panic, I gasped for breath, still in shock.

Then, just as suddenly, she was gone. She had disappeared into her room, the door slamming shut behind her. I heard gibberish coming from the other side.

Reeling from the assault, I opened my eyes, caught my breath, and forced myself to get up. I didn't cry—I couldn't. Everything happened so quickly that I needed to put myself back together again. I pulled down my polo shirt, adjusted my shorts, and tried to see myself the way I was only moments earlier. I ran into the bathroom, splashed cold water on my face, and looked into the mirror above the sink to make certain the reflection I saw was my own.

"This is me," I told myself. "This really is me."

Without drying my face, my cheeks still wet, I ran down the stairs and went outside to play. I told no one what had happened, since there was no way for me to reconcile the image of my mother with the crazed person who had attacked me. Instead, I buried it so deeply that I convinced myself that I had imagined it all. It had never occurred. Not one second of it.

On that day, I continued to play until all the other mothers called all the other girls to come home for dinner. I walked slower than usual, took the house key out from my pocket, opened our door, climbed the stairs, and said, "I'm home, Mother. Are you here? Mother, are you here?" There was no answer. There were no lights on in the apartment. I smelled no food cooking in the kitchen, and though I was still ignoring what had happened earlier, I panicked and shouted, "Mother, are you here?" I stood there alone, frozen, numb. I lost all sense of time. Moments later, when I heard Father coming up the stairs, I realized it must have been six o'clock.

As soon as he looked around and saw no sign of Mother, he went into their bedroom. A few seconds later he came out again, a pained expression on his face, and he called Dr. Andrews, whispering their conversation so I couldn't hear what he was saying. The doctor arrived at our house a few minutes later.

After some time in Mother's room and talking with Father, Dr. Andrews came out, looked at me, and said: "I gave your mother an injection to help her sleep, Linda. Don't worry." He paused and then added, "Take care, Linda, and be a good girl. Get some rest."

That question—"Mother, are you here?"—plagued me throughout her life and mine. Even when she was present in my life and doing her best to offer love and protection, those times were fleeting, punctuated with ominous unknowns.

Reminders of the sadness that filled our rooms haunted me for years, but it wasn't until thirty years later that I remembered it all. I'd been reading a newspaper article describing what a deranged mother had done to her daughter. Only then did my own memory suddenly surface. To this day, I marvel at the power of denial and the mind's ability to store unwanted memories.

Even now, with years of practice as a psychotherapist behind me and several years of my own therapy, there are times when life is relatively calm, and still I don't trust that it will last—that somehow, in some way, a storm is probably looming.

CHAPTER 12
THE MIDDLE MAN

Father and I hardly saw each other during the week. I really didn't know him. He was the man Mother said worked hard and wasn't to be bothered.

What I did know came mainly from the stories Mother told me and from what I overheard when she talked about him to her sisters or brothers. I doubt she intended to turn me against my father. Rather, I think she desperately needed an ally—anyone, even a very young daughter—to understand the pain her husband's family had caused her.

She claimed that they were old-fashioned, often insensitive, and unkind, especially when she suffered her first breakdown after Herbie was born.

"Don't think I don't know they encouraged him to leave me. Don't think I don't know that his sister Pauline was jealous of me. Until he married me, everybody called her the beauty in the family. Believe me, I often wished I was ugly, if that would have made them treat me better.

"Foolish me, marrying a man with a whole family, thinking that I'd finally have parents again," she added, her tone changed. "I was better off when I was single and independent, had a job, and was respected even though I was a boarder in a stranger's house. Then, at least, I had memories of our sweet Mama and Tateh, who didn't have the *mazel*, the luck, to survive long enough to see us all grow up and can't be here for me now when I need them, here in America."

She openly confessed feeling frightened just before her wedding, when Father demanded that she change her name from Mary, which she had been called since her arrival at Ellis Island, to Miriam. "You can't be called Mary," he said. "Mary's not a Jewish name."

"But everyone here knows me as Mary. I've gotten used to it."

"So, you'll get used to Miriam. That's a good name, a good Jewish name."

Once again, Mother buried her anger and swallowed the words flung at her. Crying, she locked herself in the bathroom and sat there, her anger and frustration having nowhere to go but inward.

She realized on their honeymoon that she had made a mistake. "At a time when I longed to feel loved and adored, my so-called husband seemed more interested in spending his time with the owners and guests at the hotel than he was in being with me," she said. Then, after a pause, she'd add, "Even when we were together, he didn't act like I imagined a man on his honeymoon would act. There was no—what you would call romance—only disappointment and inconsideration."

In the bedroom of their hotel—a room she had envisioned as looking like all the ones she'd seen in the films of American love stories—she found herself weeping for the many losses in her life, for all that she didn't have, and the sadness she'd lived with but had never spoken about to anyone.

Perhaps if my father had spent more time with me, I wouldn't have focused on all the negative things Mother had told me about him and his side of the family. He had, after all, done his best to keep us together and take care of us. He repressed his temper until the pressure of Mother's behavior forced it out in seemingly trivial incidents that frightened me.

"For God's sake," he'd shout, if someone accidently broke a glass. "Why can't people in this house be more careful?" His face would turn beet-red, and he'd slam his hand down on the kitchen table, rattling the plates.

"Please, Moish," Mother would plead. "It's only a glass. Five cents in Woolworth's. I'll get another one." He would merely sigh heavily with his eyes squeezed shut, shake his head slowly, and leave the room.

The angrier Father acted, the more anxious Mother became. The more anxious and fragile she became, the more spotless she made our apartment. The more spotless the apartment, the more pervasive the sense of peril that crept into our home, feeding Father's frustration and my fears.

On the rare occasions when Father talked about his childhood in Russia, I learned only that he was named *Mosheh*, born in 1901, the fifth of seven children. When he did mention having grown up on a farm before the war, he told us that he and his brothers rode horses bareback, milked cows, and cared for farm animals. I don't think I ever believed him entirely. None of what he described matched what I knew about the man who left the house each day in a suit, starched shirt, and a tie. He didn't seem to know anything about animals, let alone horses, to say nothing of riding them bareback.

Yet, he'd tell us, "When horses are young, they are all wild." He'd make sure to let us know that his brother, Hersh, was best at taming horses. I believed that, but never thought I knew Father any better after hearing his stories about life in Russia.

What did make sense was hearing that before he was five, Father was allowed to pray with the older boys and men in their synagogue, because he seemed to have a photographic memory and was already reading. Later, because he displayed impressive skills in mathematics, he was given a private tutor and never attended school.

All that ended abruptly at the start of World War I, when he was eleven. Father never shared many of the details of the hardships he and his family endured throughout the war. He told us that he and each of his brothers slept with guns under their pillows, as they hid in a haystack in the barn, defending the family farm. His parents had left them there and moved with his sisters to an apartment in the nearby city of Kobrin in Belarus. I suppose he told us that much because we often asked him why he had a slight tremor in his hands. He said it started when he began to sleep in that barn, clutching his gun.

In talking about the war years, Father described Kobrin as being divided in half by the Mukhavets River and the Dnieper-

Burg Canal. As the Russian army retreated and the German army approached, each on either side of the river, the civilians were caught in the middle. The Jews, frightened and in peril, gathered in front of the largest synagogue. Thinking they were the enemy army, German planes released a bomb, killing many of the town's people. Soldiers also were killed and buried fifty to a grave. "Twenty-five heads up, twenty-five heads down," Father would say. "I was watching the way it was done. That remained in my memory for life."

Some of his other stories, especially the ones about how he immigrated to the States, were almost as painful to hear as Mother's. On the ship coming to America, a young, beautiful woman who was forced to have her long red hair shaved due to a fear of lice jumped overboard, committing suicide because she felt so ashamed. Father said, "When you've seen something like that, you never forget it. That was a day I wish I never witnessed."

Although they had each faced many hardships, I've always believed that Father's life was more stable. That may have left him better able to cope with adversity after arriving in America.

During some of the quieter times, when Mother wasn't sick, I began to gain a new awareness of my father and to appreciate how he functioned in the outside world. He called himself a salesman. "The middle man," he'd say, "not the manufacturer, not the store-keeper. I'm the middle man."

I began to see him in the middle everywhere he turned. Trapped in the middle, he was unable to escape in business, in our family, and in his marriage. He remained caught between loyalties to old world European traditions and responsibilities to a wife whose problems he had no way of managing.

Occasionally, when we were on our way to visit family in the Canarsie section of Brooklyn, Father would stop at the Brooklyn Terminal Market where he and his partner rented storage space and a small office where they kept supplies of their trade: hangers, drums of chemicals, twine, and paper-goods, which they sold to what he called "dry-cleaning establishments." Usually, he just wanted to collect the mail, hoping to find a check.

As I waited, I watched the frantic activity at the market. It was a world filled with men dealing in wholesale foods, meat, fish, pickles in barrels, and ethnic delicacies. Some were in blood-stained butcher's aprons. Truckers and stackers were yelling at one another about deliveries, all of them cursing loudly, abusively. In his starched white shirt, pressed suit, and conservative tie, Father seemed out of place there, too. Even in that world he inhabited when he wasn't at home, he didn't seem to belong. He wasn't fully American and no longer totally Russian. He was truly caught in the middle.

One day when I was eleven and home from school on a holiday, Mother was having one of her episodes. I was awakened by Father coming up the stairs. He had already taken Mother to Aunt Esther's for the day, but he didn't discuss anything about her with me. He simply said that Mother was at my aunt's house and I was to come with him to his office while he took care of "some business."

A sense of excitement and privilege came over me. It was probably the very first time I'd be alone with Father. Also, because it was a holiday, the normally chaotic market would be quiet.

I watched with amazement as he unlocked a set of chains that secured the front door, and then used other keys to open the door leading into the warehouse where the paper, twine, and hangers were stored. We walked the full length of the huge, unheated storage area before climbing the stairs to the enclosed office space he shared with his partner and bookkeeper. Entering the office, he turned on the heat—a clunky, old-fashioned electric heater that sat on the floor next to his desk. I headed for his large chair and watched as he stood, sifting through mail, neatly opening envelopes with a letter opener, discarding the junk mail, carefully, compulsively, ripping each into four, six, and then eight equal pieces.

I enjoyed watching him from behind that large, mahogany desk. My eyes took in everything around me: a leather-bound calendar on top of his desk, a matching leather cup for pens and pencils just like Herb's, and a blotter with the same matching leather in each of its four corners. Then my gaze froze on a prominently placed eight-by-ten photo of my brother. It was the only picture on Father's desk.

Taking a moment to catch my breath, I found the courage to ask, "Where's a picture of me? I only see this one here of Herbie."

"Of you, I don't think I have one. I never got one of you," he said. Then he added, "Mama never gave me one." Barely apologizing, he placed the blame on Mother.

We stayed in the office for at least an hour. All the while, I thought only about the presence of Herbie's photo and the absence of mine. Father and son, the men in the family, sharing knowing glances across the dinner table, talking about the Yankees, enjoying a special relationship. I was, in the end, only the daughter—the girl Father probably believed would be as fragile and difficult as Mother was.

I wanted to cry, to kick something, or to shout my name. Yet I couldn't behave like Mother when she was sick. I couldn't allow myself to lose control. I was determined not to let Father know what I was thinking or feeling. I refused to let him know that I felt undervalued. I refused to have him look at me in that same way he looked at Mother, with that pitiful, angry face.

With no one there to protect me, I protected myself in the only way I knew. I sat up tall, fixed a smile on my face, and held back my tears.

I wondered though, if it was true that I was fated to become like Mother, or would simply be destined to remain invisible.

CHAPTER 13
BUILDING #6

I was awakened one morning, startled by a bird flapping its wings against my window. Then another sound made me sit up. It was Mother pacing aimlessly, her unslippered feet slapping the floor. There was no way for me to know whether the two sounds were separate or whether I'd been dreaming of the bird and heard Mother's footsteps.

Frightened, I forced myself to get out of bed and go into the kitchen, where I found Father seated, staring nervously across the kitchen table. The colorful cotton tablecloth, usually ironed meticulously and draped across the table, was gone. Thrown across it as a substitute was the plastic one we used only as a protector. In our normally spotless apartment, this was a clear sign that something was very wrong.

Father sat facing the doorway, staring wearily, looking nowhere and everywhere, heavy sighs punctuating the rhythmic tapping of his fingers against the tabletop. His brown checkered sports jacket was draped neatly across the back of his chair at the head of the table, but he wasn't sitting in that chair. He was seated at a peculiar angle in Herb's chair—one of the side chairs—away from the table.

Suddenly, an overwhelming, nightmarish energy charged the room. It was Mother. I caught a glimpse of her wearing a ripped, faded cotton nightgown, her face ashen, her hair unwashed, uncombed. In her bare feet and in that tattered gown, she looked shorter than her five feet three inches, her body slighter, whiter than ever. The auburn curls that normally rested softly at the nape of her neck were matted, twisted, tangled. Her sweet, smooth face that came alive with a dab of powder or a stroke of lipstick was also gone. Unblinking eyes darted wildly from object to object, eyes so dark the pupils were indistinguishable from the irises, the whites hardly visible at all. She was frightened, an ancient figure, a pitiful stranger. She was out of the room as quickly as she had entered.

Seeing her that way, I wasn't sure whether I was awake or simply unable to escape from a nightmare.

Suddenly, Father got up from his chair, grabbed Mother's arm, and, in an angry, alarming voice, said, "It's not safe for you to stay home alone today, Miriam. Let me call Dr. Andrews. Let's hear what he has to say."

Each time he spoke, his words were interrupted by a jerk of her head or a moan. With every interruption, he pleaded, "Miriam, please. Please, Miriam."

Her movements became more and more frenetic, her voice higher pitched. "I don't need a doctor," she shrieked. "I don't need to speak to nobody."

"Miriam, please go get yourself dressed. Comb your hair."

She stared vacantly across the yellow linoleum floor, whispering, "Who can I talk to? Only God can help me now, but you must make Him listen, so I can put an end to it. You'll all be better off without me. You tell Him that. To you He'll listen."

"Please, Miriam, not in front of the child," he said, not looking at me.

"Those Hitler devils. The demons. I have to get rid of them. I have to stop this torture."

I needed her to stop talking, to stop saying those words, and to take them all back.

Father told me to get dressed for school and handed me seventy-five cents to buy lunch in the cafeteria. Normally, I walked home at lunchtime and Mother served me a home-cooked meal. Asking me to eat in school meant he was going to take her to one of my aunts for the day. "You can't come home today," he said without any explanation. But I didn't really need one. I knew.

By the time I got dressed, Father had convinced Mother to put on a housedress, a pair of stockings, and her black everyday shoes. I followed as he took her by the arm and walked down the stairs with her, led her to the passenger's side of the car, waited until she was seated, and then shut and locked the door before walking back around to the driver's side. I opened the door and sat in the back. No one spoke.

I couldn't see either of their faces. Father looked straight ahead, seeming to concentrate only on his driving, not looking at Mother or saying a word to her. Mother sat slumped, crumpled, crumbling.

Neither one acknowledged me until Father double-parked in front of the entrance to my school. "Take care, Lindaleh," he said. "I'll see you later."

Mother didn't say goodbye or turn around to look at me. She just stared vacantly down at her lap. I wanted to say something to make her feel better, but no words would come. I repeated Father's words back to him. "See you later." Then, needing to believe it, I managed to add, "See you later, too, Mother."

But I didn't see her later.

No one was home when I returned from school in the afternoon. Instead, I found a note printed on the back of a brown paper lunch bag and taped to our front door. Written in large, square, block letters were the words: "GO PLAY AT A FRIEND'S HOUSE. I WILL BE HOME BY 6 O'CLOCK. YOUR FATHER."

Mother was in a hospital. I didn't see her for a week, and no one would tell me why she was there—just that she needed to be there. As usual, I asked no questions. I was, as Mother had been when she was a child in Russia, "a good girl." I learned not to ask, just as she had learned the same lesson many years before me.

Father took me to Aunt Esther's each night for dinner. He drove me to the hospital to see Mother on the first Sunday in November. It was cold, the air crisp, the sky metallic gray. We chose our clothing carefully. Father's suit was pressed, his white shirt starched, his tie knotted perfectly. My navy pleated skirt and white long-sleeved blouse with a bow at its neck matched my white anklet socks and shiny, black weekend shoes.

As we left the crowded streets of our Brighton Beach neighborhood, he clutched the steering wheel and stared at the road ahead, squinting from the sun's rays reflecting off the windshield. In the passenger's seat next to him, I gazed at the leafless trees lining Ocean Parkway. They were stripped of color, bare and unprotected. I could focus only on the frightening images and sounds from the days and nights before Mother disappeared.

We drove for nearly an hour before I saw the sign: County Hospital. Looking straight ahead, Father said, "Here, Linda, this here is where Mama's at."

Facing me was a cluster of drab, gray buildings. Dead trees stood naked and forlorn, their fallen limbs rotting on the ground amid sparse patches of brown grass. Most of the windows were barred. I couldn't imagine Mother surviving in such a place—at home, she was forever opening windows, constantly in need of fresh air.

As we left the car, my stomach tightened, my hands grew cold. Without asking permission, I clutched Father's arm, and saying nothing more, he led me toward a building with a black #6 painted on its front door.

The first person we saw inside was a man seated behind a desk at a guard's station. His large, dirty hands held a newspaper in front of his face, and the top of his balding head was the only other part of him that was visible. Father cleared his throat, coughed, then stammered, too intimidated to continue.

"We're here to see my mother, Mrs. Appleman," I said, speaking slowly, enunciating my words clearly.

"Yeah, okay," the man mumbled, without looking up from his paper. Then, sliding a clipboard out from under it, he looked quickly at a list of names. "Take the elevator to the fifth floor. To the locked ward. You'll have to wait there until whoever's on duty comes out to get her."

In the elevator, two nurses stood in a corner laughing. One of them mimicked one of her patients, saying, "Today, she thought she saw crawling spiders and gigantic rats. Last week she saw monkeys." As their laughter grew, so did my hatred for them, especially the one who spoke through lips covered in thick orange lipstick.

The elevator car lurched when the door to the fifth floor opened. I grabbed Father's hand before he pulled me out to where another guard sat in full view. The guard pointed to a row of plastic chairs, each one nailed to the floor and attached to the one next to it.

Father found us two seats. Other men sat waiting, too, almost all dressed in weekend clothes: suits, pressed shirts, ties, shoes recently shined. There was only one woman visitor. She sat in a far corner, a worried expression on her face, a son older than me holding her hand. The two of us were the only children there.

Father folded his coat, took off his hat, and placed them both neatly on his lap. Mother had always told me that he was particularly polite with strangers, more so than with any of us at home. "Outside, that's a different story," she used to say. "Outside, he's always a gentleman."

In that moment, I knew what she told me was true. And he acted as if I wasn't there. Seated next to him, I felt his right leg shake, heard the heel of his shoe tapping on the linoleum floor.

I counted its yellow and green squares. The entire floor smelled of the same nauseating Pine-Sol disinfectant that caused my head to ache whenever Mother used it at home.

The hands of the clock behind the guard's desk didn't seem to move. In that hospital, time itself was as stuck, as frozen as I was.

Father turned toward the man next to him. With his back to me, he asked, "So, what line of work are you in?"

Another man, not waiting for an answer, said, "Is this your wife's first time here? Mine's been back three times. They know me already." His voice grew weak. "It never ends."

"You think such a life a man chooses?" one asked. "It's what you're dealt. A rotten deck of cards God gives you. But you gotta play the hand…for the children, at least."

They talked as if they were the ones who were suffering, not their wives, the patients inside this terrifying place. I sat under the weight of all that I didn't understand. I thought about what Mother used to tell me, the wisdom she shared with me when she was well: "People should always be kind and considerate, Lindichkeh. They should always consider the next person's feelings."

It's hard to believe now that I never truly asked about Mother's illness and that no one thought it necessary to talk to me about it. I didn't ask what kind of hospital she was in or for how long she'd be there. I suppose I knew that such questions wouldn't be appreciated. I was as invisible at the hospital as I was at home.

Keys jangled and the door to the locked ward opened. A nurse in a starched white dress, a huge ring of keys hooked to her belt, led a group of patients shuffling behind her into the waiting room. Of the three men and nine women, each dazed and pathetic, Mother was last in line.

"Walk slowly, find your visitors," the nurse said, never turning around to face them.

Mother moved toward us. Her head was bent, and she looked totally defeated, unable to walk a straight line. The part of her face I could see was absolutely white, and a faded housedress, neither starched nor clean, hung loosely on her frail body. I'd never seen her so thin.

Father gave her an obligatory kiss on the cheek. I hugged her and tried to put my head on her shoulder, but she moved away.

Without hesitating, Father commanded, "Linda, take her! Go with her for a walk! She needs to be with you."

"With me?"

"Yeah, yeah, she'll feel better when she's with you." Wanting to believe him, I hooked arms with Mother, who did not resist me.

We followed the others. All of them were going outside to the broken wooden benches inside a courtyard with high steel fencing separating the hospital from the surrounding neighborhood.

Mother sat next to me and our bodies touched. We remained silent, her gaze vacant.

"Where am I, mamaleh?" she finally asked. Before I could answer, she continued, her speech rapid, intense: "I can't stay here anymore. Listen to me. I need to be in my own bed. You understand, don't you mamaleh? Please. Take me home. Today! Okay? Take me home today!"

"You need to be here. It's good for you here," I said, repeating words I must have heard before, but she wasn't listening.

"Mama, Mama, help me," she said, pleading with her dead mother. Then in a low, guttural voice: "Dear heavenly Father, show me the way." With that, she grabbed my arm, pinching it tightly, whispering, "Please mamaleh, please take me home!"

"I can't."

"Please, I promise I'll be good..."

"Mother..."

"I hate these doctors, the nurses—they're all terrible. They're mean. Don't leave me here! Please, mamaleh, you can't leave me here."

I didn't know how to respond. I tried to sound grown-up. "I can't take you home. You need to be where doctors can help you." What else could I say?

Some of the other patients frightened me even more than Mother. They stared without an awareness of what they were looking at, appearing to see through and beyond people and walls, into a world visible only to themselves.

Most disturbing was the story of the wife of one of the other men in the waiting area. Her husband repeated the same story every time we saw him. "Imagine," he droned, "she thinks she's paralyzed, so she never gets out of bed." I tried not to think about how it could be possible for anyone to believe she was incapable of moving when doctors insisted she could. Instead, I forced myself to think about my friends, about playing stoop ball and Monopoly and going swimming. I couldn't stop myself, though, from wondering what was in store for me. Would there be a day when doctors wouldn't believe me? Worse still, would I ever become like Mother, trapped in a hospital like this one?

Mother was talking to herself, rocking gently back and forth. "If only Mama and Tateh were alive, I wouldn't be here. Not here, Lindaleh. Not in a place like this. They would take care of me. No one should ever be here. Not here. Not anyone."

After such visits, I'd awaken in the middle of the night stricken with terror. In the darkness, I'd call out for Father, who'd get out of bed and come down the hall to my room. "It's all right, Lindichkeh. Everything's all right. I'm here."

He'd ask if I wanted him to sit in my room until I fell back asleep, but I was too embarrassed to say yes, so he'd leave silently. Simply seeing him was comforting, though, even when I was unable to fall back asleep. I never did believe everything was really all right—or would be again.

In the days before she disappeared, being home with Mother had felt unsafe, and yet being with her at the hospital seemed even worse. After several weeks she was no longer as restless and grew more coherent, but she was unable to censor what she told me.

In that hospital she revealed how she feared for her life. In the hospital she talked about whatever came into her mind. "After I fell asleep one night, another patient wandered into my room and crept into my bed. I felt sorry for him afterwards," she added. "He was probably *mishugah* from the medication they give. He's not a bad soul. He didn't mean any harm. He just thought my room was his room, and he came in by mistake. I had to be the lucky one."

"Imagine," she continued, "I finally fall asleep after hours of tossing and turning. Then next to me I feel this body. I think it's your Papa. Then I remember I'm here in this miserable hospital. So, I called out for the nurse who, of course, took her jolly time in coming. Once she did, he was gone already.

"'Okay, Miriam,' she said, 'go back to sleep. Sam is sorry. He didn't mean to scare you. He's back in his own room now.' Then she leaves. But the rest of the night I don't sleep. Some place I'm in. A regular Waldorf Astoria, huh?"

That tiny hint of humor raised my hopes for her recovery, but the moment was fleeting. A second later, she rambled again, tearing at her hands, their skin rough, her nails ragged. Could this be my mother who bathed her hands in Jergens lotion before going to bed each night, the mother who had soft, pretty fingers with beautifully manicured nails?

Then she began to pinch my arm. I pretended it didn't hurt, but I could no longer be alone with her and had to bring her back to Father. When he saw us approaching, he stood, put on his overcoat, and quickly readied himself to leave.

"We'll come back in a few days," he told Mother. Then, looking almost as pained and helpless as she did, he begged, "Please, Miriam, eat the meals. Get some rest. You know that always helps." His tone was gentle, his words patronizing.

As though we weren't right next to her, Mother straightened, arched her back, and gazed into the distance through one of the waiting room's barred windows. When we were about to leave, she turned toward Father with eyes narrowed, hostile, piercing. "You don't know what's best for me. You, my so-called husband. You who put me here!"

Defeated and barely audible, he whispered, "Miriam, please..."

"You are my enemy!" she hissed fiercely.

Her eyes dark and wild, she turned, staring at me, imploring me, "Linda..." but her voice trailed off. She was already being escorted back to the locked ward. I wanted desperately to stop looking at her, but I needed to see her. Some part of me wanted to go with her. I couldn't move. Is this how a paralyzed woman feels, I wondered as the metal door clanged shut behind her.

"Come. It's time now to go," Father said.

I stood still, my eyes riveted on the metal door, imagining Mother somewhere behind it.

"Linda, come," Father said, taking my hand.

We left together, returning to the familiar world outside.

CHAPTER 14
A CONFLICT OF LOYALTIES

I curled my cold hands into the pockets of my loden green winter coat as we walked to the parking lot. Father fiddled with the keys in his pocket. It was easy to spot our car in the crowded lot. Spanking clean, the shiny black hood reflected the deep blue of the late afternoon sky. Father opened the door of the passenger's side and waited for me to tuck in my coat before shutting my door and walking around to the driver's side.

After starting the engine, he kept it in neutral for several minutes. He never raced the motor. "A car is a delicate machine," he reminded me. "You have to take very good care of it. You have to pay attention to it." Father took particular pride in keeping his car in perfect working condition, washing and waxing it regularly, checking the oil, keeping the gas tank full at all times.

When we began the trip home, I rolled down my window, welcoming the refreshing cold air against my cheeks.

"We'll eat out tonight, Linda," Father said, breaking the silence. "At Dubrow's Cafeteria. You know, the restaurant you like, the one on Kings Highway."

I nodded.

"Tomorrow, I'll give you money. You'll buy two pieces of white fish to bake for dinner, with spaghetti. You'll make the chocolate pudding for dessert. It'll be easier, if we stick to Mama's routine. Mondays and Thursdays, dairy. Okay?"

"Sure," I said.

Until then he hadn't spoken to me about Mother. Suddenly, he was talking about my cooking, unaware that Mother never let me help, let alone prepare an entire meal. Dinner was always ready when he came home.

The next day after school, I bought the food with the money he gave me. When I got home, I set the kitchen table. I folded a paper napkin so that the triangular point faced the dinner plate, placed a fork on top of the napkin, a knife and dessert spoon to the right of each plate. I thought that was how Mother did it. It looked right.

After completing my homework, I put on Mother's apron, doubling the waist up and then tying the cloth belt around twice or three times before making a bow. Then I did what I'd always seen her do and what Father expected. At 5:30, I took the fish out of its paper wrapping, ran it under cold water, put it in our Pyrex baking dish, and sprinkled each piece with salt and pepper. I scraped two carrots, rinsed them, cut them into chunks and placed them alongside the fish, adding a glass of cold water to the pan. In a separate pot, I boiled water and threw in #8 spaghetti strings, which I'd broken into halves, quarters and then eighths.

The spaghetti was the easiest to prepare. I kept swirling it around with a fork, and after twenty minutes, I transferred it from the pot into the spaghetti strainer, running cold water over it before returning it to the pot on the stove. While the spaghetti warmed again, I put plenty of butter on top and waited for it to melt. We never ate it with store-bought sauce, as I knew other families did. We liked ours with butter and sometimes just plain ketchup.

To get the oven to work, I had to light a match to ignite the flame. This was the hardest part. I had never lit a match before. I knew that Mother wouldn't approve, but I didn't stop to think of what she might say. I pictured myself as though I were her, copying her movements as I remembered them. I struck the match, watched it flare up, and placed the end that was lit exactly where I thought she always placed it. There was no time to be frightened. I know now that it was sheer luck that I didn't set the house on fire.

Once I heard the same clicking sound that I heard whenever Mother lit the oven, I felt relieved that it was on and working. Then I reached for a box of My-T-Fine chocolate pudding in the cupboard and was grateful for the printed instructions on the side of the package. I poured two cups of milk into the dry chocolate powder, mixed it all up with our special wooden chocolate pudding spoon, and cooked it in one of Mother's small dairy pots.

When it started to boil, I stopped stirring and shut off the flame. After pouring half-cup servings into four small glass bowls, I did the one thing Mother always allowed me to do: I left some in the pot for scraping and licking. There was no taste in the world like the warm, sweet taste of that thick chocolate scraped off the insides of the pot.

When Father came home, he sat in his chair at the head of the kitchen table and told me I was a good girl. "Just like Mama,

Lindaleh. You cook just like Mama. Very good. Just like Mama, I mean it."

By restoring order to my life, Father helped me feel safe again. Yet that safety excluded Mother, the person I needed and loved more than anyone else.

Except for the days when I was together with Father in temple, he'd been the one person in the family with whom I'd spent the least amount of time. Now, with Mother in the hospital and Herb no longer home, I felt disloyal living alone with him. After all, Mother had called him her enemy.

Yet I was grateful for his company and appreciated him as I never had before. Father worked hard, unlike Mother, who was unable to concentrate, even on simple tasks. I could count on him to come home each night at the exact time that he said he would, and I looked forward to planning meals together and discussing household chores.

With Mother gone, he took an interest in my life and talked to me about articles he read in the newspapers. He was affectionate, and I began to enjoy being with him. At the same time, I felt conflicted about it, which added to my anxiety.

"So, Lindichkeh," he'd say. "How was school? Any fire drills like last week when you had to run out without even time to get your coat?"

"No drills today."

"And homework? With arithmetic I can help you, but geography don't ask me. Maps I never learned how to read. East, west, north, south, who can figure it out? But arithmetic, ask me anything."

"It's okay. I didn't have much homework today. I even had time to go to Audrey's house after school. Her mother gave us milk and homemade chocolate chip cookies."

"That's nice. I'm glad."

It felt good to have him ask about my day, though the contrast between him and Mother continued to haunt me. Before, their roles in my life had been clearly defined. Now, everything was changing. While Mother used to be loving and Father distant, Father was now attentive and Mother was gone. For years afterward, I believed that gaining something good came at a painful cost.

Most frightening was the knowledge that she and the other women in the hospital were considered burdens by their families. If I knew anything, it was that I was not going to become like any of them.

I promised myself never to depend on anyone for my freedom or my health, and never to be a victim or suffer the humiliation Mother experienced. And I would never have a husband who seemed to be my enemy. I would not grow up to become like Mother.

Repeating that promise to myself became a nightly ritual. Though I shared it with no one, it was reassuring. I went to school, did my homework, studied, got good grades, went to the movies with my girlfriends, and seemed, even to myself, to be happy.

Yet, during those times when Mother slipped away and life in our family continued to be unpredictable, I, too, slipped into silence—hiding the truth from myself and from others. I thought I was in control, but I didn't know that such control gave a false face to the complexity of my fears, denying me the freedom to play or to laugh without expecting a price to be paid for any pleasures. I needed to believe the world was safe, but I never truly convinced myself that it was.

CHAPTER 15
THE DRAMATIC WORKSHOP

A week before Herb was to leave for his sophomore year at Harvard, he lay on his bed at home reading while I folded laundry on mine. Mother had been home for a while, and she was feeling better.

Suddenly, he closed his book, sat up, and stared at me.

"Lin, we have to talk," he said.

"What is it?" My heart skipped as I remembered our talk before his freshman year.

"Since I've been away at school," he began, then stopped, folded his arms across his chest, and looked at the floor, then back up at me with a pained expression.

"What?" I asked, never before having known him to stumble for words.

"Well, whenever I get one of your letters, they're so sweet. I just love them. But then I start to think about you, and I feel guilty."

"About what?"

"About your being home alone. Alone with Mom and Dad. Especially because I know Mom had a rough winter this year."

She sure did, I thought. We all had a rough winter, but Herb hadn't been there. And when he called, he'd only asked to speak to me once. So what did he know about what it was like for me to hear Mother talking to herself? Or to God? To see her in the hospital? What could he say to change what had already happened?

"Knowing you were here without me," he continued, "well, it made me sad."

"It's okay."

"Yeah, but it's not okay with me. I know what Mom's like when she's sick." His expression changed to one of anger.

"You mean when Father takes her to the doctor for treatments?"

"Yeah. The treatments." He paused, sighed. "Dad called me one night in my dorm. Did you know that?" he continued. "He wanted me to come home because I was the one who often took her to the doctor. But I couldn't. I had to study for exams, Lin. I just couldn't come home."

That was the first time I'd ever heard of Herb's having taken Mother for her treatments. Later, I would come to know just how much Father relied on him when Herb was only a boy.

I had heard Father's end of some of their weekly telephone conversations: "You shouldn't know from what's going on. It's the same story all over again. Do I have to tell you?"

I never heard the details, because I didn't want to be caught listening, so I remained the outsider, understanding better than ever what Mother meant the few times she had talked to me about how differently Father acted toward me because I was "the girl." What Father shared with Herb was not what he shared with me.

"Lin, I felt crappy knowing I wasn't here for you."

I wanted to tell him of the enormous loss we had felt when he'd gone away to school, but I couldn't. Mother in her way, Father in his, had missed him desperately. For me, it was the loss of a friend, ally, and protector. With him gone and Mother in the hospital, I was deserted by them both. The more I thought about it, the more I realized how lonely I had been since he had left. Tears I'd held back for so long ran down my cheeks.

"But you couldn't be here. I understand," I heard myself saying.

"Well, if I could, I would have taken you out after school when Mom was either at Aunt Esther's, or we could have gone to a movie or the library, anything to get you out of the house when she was sick."

"It's not so much that I missed doing stuff with you during the day. It's just, well, the nights were scary," I confessed.

"I'm so sorry, kiddo." He sat next to me on my bed and put his arm around my shoulders. At his touch, a sob caught my breath. He pulled me close and gave me a bear hug and a kiss on my cheek.

Not wanting to upset him, I said, "Most of the time it's really okay."

"Listen, I have an idea," he said. "One of my roommates has a kid sister who takes all sorts of interesting classes in Philadelphia—dancing and acting, in particular. Is that something you'd like?"

"Acting classes? For the stage, you mean?"

He nodded. "There's a good school in Manhattan. I want to talk to the folks about it. They probably won't like the idea at first, but let me handle it. Whadda you say, kiddo?"

"You suppose I could ever become a real actress?"

"I don't know, but what's important is that it would get you out of Brighton. You could make some new friends."

I smiled, shrugged and said, "Sure, okay."

He gave me another hug and went to speak to Father, who was sitting in the kitchen reading and drinking a glass of tea. I leaned against the doorpost of my room, listening to their conversation.

"I've been thinking about Lin a lot these days, Dad. She's very shy, you know."

"Linda's shy?" Father said, sipping his tea.

"Especially around adults. And I think she'd feel better about herself if she had more poise. Anyway, I have an idea, something I think would be good for her."

"You and your ideas!"

"Just put the paper down for a minute and listen, okay?"

"Okay, already," Father conceded. I heard more rustling of the paper. Then it stopped. With that, I knew if anyone could convince him, Herb was the one to do it.

"I think she'd really enjoy being a part of a theater program. So, here's what I propose," he said authoritatively. "She's pretty and smart, and it would give her confidence and make her feel less shy. Most of all, it would get her out of the house. She's home alone with Mom too much. She deserves to have some fun."

"Fun? She has fun when she plays with the other girls on the block."

"Yeah, but I'm not talking about that kind of fun. This is important. You work all day. I'm away in Cambridge. And, Mom, well, you know, Mom is Mom."

A pause between them followed, before my father said, "Why does she need professional? She's been taking little dance classes since she was in first grade. Costs a pretty penny, I bet."

"These are different. She'll love the classes, and she'll love reading plays and performing on stage. Whenever I've taken her to the theater, she gets so excited when the curtain goes up. She gets a real kick out of watching the actors and actresses."

"So you want your sister should become an actress? Please, don't go and put funny ideas into her head," Father said, before calling out to Mother in the other room. "Miriam, I need you to hear about your son's idea for your daughter."

After hearing Father's version of what Herb told Father, Mother's response was, "Our Linda, an actress? Oy, Herbie, Herbie, what else do you got up your sleeve?"

"Well, wasn't it you, Mom, who named her after an actress?"

With a slight giggle and a lift in her voice, she admitted, "You remember that? Yeah, yeah. We needed a name with the letter 'L' after your grandfather, Lazer. So, I myself picked Linda for her English name. I wanted her to be beautiful like the actress, Linda Darnell."

Herb kept at it. "I found a school in Manhattan called The Dramatic Workshop. I called and they're willing to interview her this Saturday morning at eleven. She wants to go. Can you drive her there, Dad?"

Mother and Father looked at one another and, as often happened, in the end they deferred to Herb because he was Herb: the past mayor of his elementary school, the president of his high school, and the first person in our extended family to go out of town to an Ivy League school on scholarship.

So they took his advice, and though none of us knew exactly what to expect, they agreed to take me into the city for an audition.

❧

I wore a freshly pressed nylon blouse, a pleated navy skirt, new bobby socks, and my black, weekend shoes. Father buttoned the jacket of his best suit, checked his tie in the mirror, and shined his shoes with special care. Mother put on her navy suit and stood nervously holding her holiday hat in one hand and her white gloves in the other. Father had washed and polished our Pontiac sedan the day before, and I sat in the back seat as we drove into the city.

Everything thrilled me as we rode into Manhattan, especially the towering skyscrapers and the theaters and the department-store windows with their elegantly dressed mannequins. My excitement peaked the moment we drove from 42nd Street onto Broadway. Father was skeptical about the whole idea, but he perked up when he found a parking space on 50th Street, proudly announcing, "I'm a lucky man. Today I don't have to give no money to no parking garage."

With a bounce to his stride, he led Mother and me to the Capitol Theatre. He clearly knew his way around the city better than we did.

I tingled with anticipation when I saw the huge theater building on Broadway between 51st and 52nd streets. Herb had told me that Marlon Brando, the actor every girl was talking about, had been one of its recent graduates, and that the workshop was founded by a famous European actress and director, Madame Piscator.

Inside the building, we rode an elevator to the third floor. The elevator opened into a small waiting room, each wall covered with posters of theater productions from major cities around the world.

I squeezed Mother's hand tightly, hoping she was sharing the thrill of the moment with me.

A woman seated behind a desk in an office facing the waiting room stood to greet us. We were shocked to see how tiny she was. Father's eyes twinkled in a way that they did whenever he was about to tell a joke. Then he flashed one of his broad smiles at me, and I had to control myself from laughing out loud.

The lady extended a hand to Mother and Father. "How do you do," she said in a surprisingly deep voice, with a Russian accent.

Father smiled and responded with his salesman's charm, "How do you do? I am Mr. Appleman. This here is my wife, Mrs. Appleman, and this is our daughter, Linda."

"I am Madame Tolstoy," she said, emphasizing *Madame*. "I am the person who selects the students for the great actress and director of our school, Madame Piscator."

While I had never heard the name Piscator, I felt certain that being interviewed by Madame Tolstoy was a good omen. Herb had just read the novel *War and Peace*, by an author named Leo Tolstoy, and he had told me all about it.

"You, please," she motioned to my parents, "have a seat, while I talk to your young lady here."

She seemed friendly, but I couldn't stop myself from staring at her clothes. They were unlike any I had ever seen: a dark green, two-piece suit with an extra-long skirt, a zebra-striped blouse, stockings that weren't skin-colored nylons like I was used to seeing, but black with a mesh design in them, and tiny, red, pointy high-heeled pumps. Most impressive of all, though, was her green felt hat, with its long, multi-colored feather jutting off to one side.

She motioned for me to follow her into her office, leaving Mother and Father to find seats for themselves. Glancing over my shoulder, I saw the mixed expressions of hope and concern on both their faces.

Once alone with Madame, my eyes bulged with excitement. My legs, too, felt rubbery.

"So, my young lady," she said, looking straight into my eyes from underneath the cocked part of her feathered hat, "you wish to study here with us. Why?"

I stared back, not knowing how to respond. I thought there must be a right answer, but I didn't know what it was, so I remained silent.

In an obvious attempt to help, she asked, "Well, do you wish to be an actress?"

"I don't know," I said, "but my brother, he goes to Harvard, and, well, it was his idea. He thinks I'd really like it here."

"And why is that?"

Again, not knowing what to say, I began with Herb's reasons.

"He told my parents he thinks I'm too shy, but I think it's because he knows how much I love the theater and how wonderful it would be to attend a school where I could go on a stage and feel what it's like to be a real actress."

"What plays have you seen?"

"A few musicals, and I'm hoping to see *The Diary of Anne Frank*."

"Are you willing to spend time at home memorizing lines from plays that we cast our students in?"

"Sure," I said.

"And are you a good reader? Do you like to read?"

"I just finished reading *Sister Carrie*. It was very sad, and I cried through most of the book. But it was great. The more I read, the more I felt like I was Carrie. I told my English teacher I think Theodore Dreiser is probably the greatest writer in the world."

"Good, good, we like intelligent students, ones who read. Here, take this book, turn to, let's see, try page three, and read me the first two little paragraphs."

My hands trembled slightly as I held the book, but I was determined to read aloud as clearly as I could. The passage she had chosen was from one of the first pages in Charles Dickens' *David Copperfield*.

"*My mother was sitting by the fire, that bright, windy March afternoon, very timid and sad, and very doubtful of ever coming alive out of the trial that was before her, when lifting her eyes as she dried them, to the window opposite...*"

I read through until the end of the page.

"You read well. Good expression. A nice voice. A pretty face. And you walk gracefully. Call your parents in to join us."

When I went out to get them, Father was sitting with his hat in his lap. Mother's straw hat was in hers, and she was nervously twisting one of her white gloves. But she still managed to smile as I invited them both in.

"Please sit," Madame said, pointing to a small sofa. "You have yourselves a very lovely young lady here."

Much to my amazement, Mother, who was usually silent in the presence of strangers, questioned Madame with a giggle, "You think our Linda can become an actress?" Her eyes opened wider than usual.

"I think if she works hard, she'll be a good student. But tell me, when your son called, he said it might be a problem for you to pay the tuition. Would a fifty percent discount—forty dollars a month, ten dollars a week, instead of twenty—be something you could manage?"

"Probably," Father said, staring down at the thinly carpeted floor beneath his feet. "That is, if you think our Linda is right for this here school. Then, we'll work it out."

"Her reading was intelligent. And we like to encourage students who are enthusiastic. So my answer to you is, yes. Definitely yes." She paused, and then concluded our meeting. "It was good to meet you. I'm sure I will see you again."

Looking in my direction, she continued, "Linda, the boys and girls in your class will be from twelve to fourteen years old. I do not know if anyone is from Brooklyn, but you will see. I believe you will get along well with all of them. They are fine, interesting young people, just like you, my dear."

She ended by saying, "I'm sure you will not be disappointed studying here. The new term begins two weeks from today. Classes start promptly at ten o'clock. At noon, you will have one hour for lunch, and classes will resume until three."

With the opportunity to leave Brighton Beach for something special, just for me, something that fed the fantasy of being on stage, another world seemed to beckon, and I felt my life was about to change.

Father drove me to my first day of classes. The teachers introduced themselves, telling us about their careers in the theater. Then each of us, seven girls and two boys, had to say why we had come to study at The Workshop.

André spoke first. His accent was wonderfully seductive. "I'm thirteen. I was born in France, and I have been living in New York since I was ten. My father works at the United Nations, where I attend school and act in all their productions. My drama teacher suggested I come here to study."

Jerry said he was twelve and from Long Island. He looked older because he was tall, with thick, curly blond hair brushed into a pompadour, which made him look even taller. "I've always enjoyed entertaining at parties, doing magician's tricks, and my uncle thinks I'd be a good actor."

Then Barbara from the Bronx, Carol from Connecticut, Sandy, Judy, and Marcia—each from Manhattan—and Lori from New Jersey all said something about themselves. I was the only one from Brooklyn, and when it was my turn, I repeated what I'd told Madame Tolstoy, saying that my older brother found out about the school, and I was very excited about starting classes.

Lori's story was the only one that was truly different. She told us that her family had just returned from a summer in England, where her mother had directed a play. She'd been able to help backstage with the costumes and sets. "I've been around the theater all my life," she said, before adding, "I want to learn more about acting. I want to be an actress. My sister's already a dancer. She performs on her toes."

If each of them, especially Lori, hadn't been so friendly, I would have felt intimidated, but I never did. We were serious during class time, but from the very first day, when we ate lunch together at the corner soda fountain at Whelan's Drug Store, sitting on high, swivel stools, ordering grilled cheese sandwiches with ice cream sundaes and imitating the foreign accents of each of our teachers, we laughed and talked easily with one another about the plays we were assigned to read and the parts we had been given.

After the first few weeks, I told Father he didn't have to drive me anymore. I could go alone. It would be easy enough to walk the five blocks along Brighton Beach Avenue to the elevated subway station.

Each Saturday, I strutted across the platform, stood in a studied, theatrical pose, held my green leatherette hatbox, and waited for the BMT Express train, my escape from Brooklyn.

I was seldom the only child traveling alone. Subways were safe then, especially since it was the same conductor each week sticking his head out the window as the train rolled into the station, saying hello, recognizing me from the previous Saturday. Then, I'd sit in the first car, right behind his compartment. Once seated, I unzipped my hatbox with my leotards, tights, slippers, and black-and-white speckled notebooks arranged neatly inside, and took out one of my books, usually the one for elocution class, to practice the correct way of pronouncing words and do breathing exercises to ready myself for class. The train would roar north to Sheepshead Bay, Kings Highway, and through the flat stretch of Brooklyn into Manhattan.

I was probably the only student on scholarship, but I don't think any of the other kids knew. When we weren't in our leotards and tights, our street clothing was similar and casual: turtleneck sweaters and blue jeans. It was our overcoats that were different. Barbara wore a real fur coat made especially for her, she told us, because her grandfather was a furrier who designed it himself. Lori's coat was a soft, camel-colored cashmere, and the others had equally expensive-looking ones. Mine was a navy blue pea jacket, one that I'd bought in Cohen's General Store on Brighton Beach Avenue.

Though I liked each of them, Lori and Barbara were the two girls I spoke with the most. I did think André was very smart and handsome, but when his French mother called to invite me to a soirée, saying that her son really liked me, I was too embarrassed to talk with him after that. I never did go to their soirée, not that I even knew what a soirée was. I lied and said I had to do something with my family and couldn't attend.

Jerry held a special fascination for us girls. We decided that he had a peculiar condition, because the palms of his hands were always stained yellow. We never found out why, but Lori, Barbara, and I couldn't help but laugh about him behind his back, comparing the degree of yellow from one week to the next and howling uncontrollably as we did so.

In drama class, we performed scenes from *Little Women*, *The Diary of Anne Frank*, and Shakespeare's *Twelfth Night*. I loved acting out parts, pretending to be someone I wasn't. The only time I felt uneasy was when one of the teachers picked on someone in a way that seemed unfair. Most often, that someone was Lori, but she didn't seem to mind as much as I did. "Because my mother's a director, they think I should know everything," she said.

To the teacher, she'd say, "I'll try that again. I think I know what you want me to do." Then, she did try again, doing it a different way. She concentrated and worked hard to do what was requested. I couldn't understand how she could be so brave.

Although I continued to attend Hebrew school from 3:30 to 5:30, Monday through Thursday, my quest for God in temple on Saturdays became less compulsive. My days at the Workshop became more important, a time to explore imagined truths on stage and discover new ways to express myself.

Our lunches at Whelan's Drug Store and the train rides into and out of the city were as much a part of the pleasure of each Saturday as the classes themselves. Every week, I'd pretend that I was about to be discovered. A famous casting agent would notice me reading a script and invite me to audition for the New York stage or fly me to Hollywood, where I'd be offered a screen test. It didn't matter that it never happened. I trusted that the magic moment would occur. Someone would want me one day and take me away from Brighton—I just didn't know when that moment would be.

I fantasized about it then and well into adolescence. It was the adrenaline rush that sustained me throughout the week from Sunday through Friday, when I contended with the real drama at home. There, I had no script to follow and no words for what I was experiencing. Unable to improvise, I usually retreated to my room, sensing the secret of Mother's illness, knowing things I didn't know I knew, knowing things I didn't want to know.

At one of our yearly performances for an audience of parents and talent scouts, I played Meg in a scene from *Little Women*. When Madame Piscator gave us notes afterward, she spoke about that scene.

"You were all good," she said. "The scene went well, but there was only one moment worth talking about." Pointing to Carole, an aspiring actress who was supposed to have been knitting during the scene, she said, "You dropped your yarn, Carole. You became flustered and left it on the floor. In real life, no one would do that. But, ah! Linda saw it happen. She remained in character and did something about it. She picked it up, and as she spoke her lines, she handed it to you and went on with the scene. You see girls, that's acting. Good work, Linda."

I enjoyed the compliment, but wasn't sure why Madame found what I'd done to be so unusual. To me, it was the most natural thing to do. I'd always felt the need to be ready to rescue a moment, a person, if only I had the chance. That was a lesson I didn't need to learn at drama school.

On stage, in that world of make-believe, I had the opportunity and seized it. I could act. It was easy for me to understand the mind and heart of complex fictional characters. Playing Joan of Arc was easy. Playing Meg was easier still. Being Linda, understanding myself and making sense of my world at home, was a far trickier role, and one that was far less rewarding.

CHAPTER 16
THROUGH LORI'S EYES

In May 1952, before our summer break, I invited Lori to come home with me for a sleepover. Her parents gave her permission to leave school with me the following Saturday, as long as someone could drive her back to Manhattan on Sunday so she could take the bus home to New Jersey. Father said it wouldn't be a problem.

After class the next week, we boarded the elevated BMT train and headed for Brooklyn. As we sat next to one another, she confessed that she'd never been to Brooklyn before and had ridden the subway only a couple of times.

"I really like this ride," she said, as the train rolled out of Manhattan. Looking through the window, her elbow resting on its sill, she was able to see Brooklyn's flat landscape with section after section of small row houses, along with clothes drying on lines in people's backyards.

"The streets are all so neat and cute," she said.

"I guess they are," I said, never having seen it that way before.

When we arrived at the Brighton station, I ushered her down the long flight of stairs to the street. From Mrs. Stahl's Famous

Knishes at the corner of Coney Island Avenue to my house on Brighton 2nd Street, Brighton Beach Avenue bustled with activity.

Lori kept looking at the elevated train tracks above, as well as into all the stores we passed along the way. "I've never been any place where so much is going on."

I smiled at her excitement and appreciated her giggling at my imitation of how the storekeepers spoke. As we continued to walk toward my house, we could hear the elevated trains whistling and roaring, moving through Brighton toward their final destination, the last stop in Coney Island.

As we turned the corner onto my street, Lori said, "I can't believe you live so close to the ocean." Then she asked if we could walk to the beach before going to my house. I wanted to please her, so I agreed. We crossed Brighton Beach Avenue, walked the block and a half toward the entrance to the beach, passing the park where I hung out with my friends on hot summer nights. Since it was still daylight, the park was packed with kids and their families.

Lori stared at them all. "I don't think I've ever seen so many people outside in one place. Ever."

"Really?" I said. "It's even more crowded in the middle of the summer when it's too hot for people to stay home. We all come out here to the park or to the beach, and sometimes even spend entire nights on the beach."

Then we took off our socks and shoes, and I led her through the shortcut to Bay #5. We walked underneath the boardwalk where it was dark and the sand wonderfully cool between our toes. The rays from the sun allowed us to see through the spaces between the slats of the boards above, and every now and then we saw people's feet or heard them talking as they passed overhead.

Since it wasn't yet summer, there weren't many people on the beach and even fewer in the ocean, but that didn't seem to matter to Lori. She was thrilled just standing there with the wide expanse of the beach in front of us. Because she was happy, so was I.

"I love the ocean. I could just sit here and look out at it all day. You're really lucky, Linda. I just love being here."

We sat silently at the edge of the beach, the damp sand beneath us. After a moment, I replied, "I guess I am lucky."

Tiny waves whispered, but the water only got our toes wet. When Lori said, "I could stay here forever," I suddenly realized an hour had probably passed since we'd gotten off the train. I didn't want her to see Mother anxious or Father angry, so I quickly said, "We'd better leave now. My folks are probably waiting for us. If you want, we can come back later today or tomorrow morning."

On the way home, we passed my friend Big Linda's house and Lillian's, too. "Lillian lives with her parents and two sisters in the basement of that house," I said, pointing to Lillian's apartment. "They're not Jewish, but they're very nice. I think they're Irish, and their mother's a nurse. She works at night, so Lillian and her sisters all know how to cook and clean. It's sad in a way because their apartment is very dark inside. They can only see people's feet walking by when they look out of their windows, just like when we were underneath the boardwalk. But, they never complain. Lillian's big sister, Beverly, is like a mother, really, and sometimes she invites me to have supper with them. She bakes fish a lot and serves it with mashed carrots and potatoes that she whips up with tons of butter."

In my eagerness to tell Lori everything about my world in Brighton—a world that clearly seemed alien to her—I realized I was talking too much. She had stopped listening and was staring curiously at everything around us.

As we approached my house, #3051, I saw Mother's head leaning out the window of our front room. I was right. She had been waiting for us.

"Linda? I was beginning to worry," she said. "Come upstairs and bring your friend with you."

Lori waved to Mother from the street and shouted up, "Hello, Mrs. Appleman. I'm Lori."

Just then, a train whistled from the elevated tracks along the Avenue. "God," Lori said. "How do you sleep with the noise of that whistle?"

"Funny, I don't really hear it. I guess I'm used to it."

When I saw Lori looking at our house, I told her that all of us who lived inside were tenants. "An awful family owns the house. I hardly ever see them, but they're really mean. My father pays the rent a few days earlier than he has to each month, so they won't yell at him."

To get to our apartment's door, we had to climb the ten steps of the outside stoop, open the front door to the house, walk past the tiny mailroom area, and through the hallway to our door leading upstairs. I took out my key, opened the door, and pointed the way for Lori to go first.

As soon as we walked up the eighteen steps to the top of the stairway, Mother said to Lori, "Hello, dear. Put your suitcase in Linda's room on Herbie's bed. Linda, show her where the bed is, and then come into the kitchen. You'll have a little snack."

Before going into my room, I gave Lori a second's worth of a tour, pointing to the bathroom at the top of the staircase, then my room to its right followed by the kitchen, my parents' bedroom, and the fourth room, the living room, or "parlor" as Mother called it. Its windows were the only ones that faced the front of the house.

Once inside my room, Lori asked if she could hang up her clothes. Her case was packed with incredible precision. Everything was folded in the same way that clothes look on the shelves of department stores. I made room in my closet for the two outfits she'd brought, and watched as she placed a pair of pressed pink pajamas at the foot of the bed, on top of the white chenille bedspread.

"Is it okay to leave my case here at the foot of the bed, or do you want me to put it someplace else?"

"No, that's fine," I said, knowing there wasn't any other place for her to put it.

When we entered the kitchen, Lori spoke to Mother before taking a cookie. "Thank you, Mrs. Appleman. The cookies look really delicious. Did you make them?"

"Oh, no, dear. I'm not much of a baker. These here cookies come from Sophie Kaplan's bakery shop down the street. You must have passed her store when you were walking up the block."

"I saw so many shops and stores, I don't remember. But thanks, anyway."

When Lori asked to be excused for a moment, Mother said, "She must come from a very good family. What manners. A real young lady."

I was happy to hear Mother speak so glowingly about Lori, but I wasn't surprised. I loved all my girlfriends in Brighton, but I didn't think any of us spoke to grown-ups the way Lori did.

In the hours before Mother served dinner, we waited in my room. The windows were half open, and warm breezes swept over us as we rested on top of our beds, two feet apart from one another, chatting and giggling about some of the boys at the Workshop.

At six o'clock Mother called us to the kitchen. Father was seated when we entered the room. He introduced himself to Lori, then kissed me on my cheek and asked, "So, how was your day in the city, Lindichkeh? Lori, Linda says you're from New Jersey. You'll forgive me for making a joke, but every time I go to Jersey I have to go over the highway from New York, and, oh, boy, does it stink from oil." He giggled and paused. "I don't mean to be insulting. It's just that's how I always think of New Jersey. Stinking from the smell of oil. I bet where you live, you don't smell the oil."

"No," she said, "we don't." Lori didn't seem annoyed, though. "I'm sorry you don't really know New Jersey better, Mr. Appleman. Obviously, I don't know it all that well, either," she said with a laugh, "because I don't know any places that smell like oil. But your story's funny, anyway."

I was embarrassed, however, and wondered why Father always needed to tell that story whenever he talked about New Jersey.

Mother's dinner that night was cantaloupe followed by baby lamb chops with mashed potatoes and string beans, a green salad, and applesauce for dessert. With each dish she served, Lori thanked her and said how delicious everything was. She also asked if she could help Mother serve.

"It's a small kitchen we have, and it's not as though I have to walk to Europe in order to bring the dishes to the table," Mother said. "And besides, dear, you're a guest. So, sit and relax. Lamb chops are Linda's favorite, so I hope you like them, too."

"Oh, I'm enjoying everything. You're a very good cook, Mrs. Appleman."

Looking at Father, Mother said, "You see Moish, Linda and Herbie aren't the only ones who appreciate my cooking."

"What are you talking? I always tell you how good your food is!"

Hearing Father compliment Mother in Lori's presence made the conversation so pleasant our family seemed almost normal.

Lori and I put our dishes in the sink after we ate, but Mother forbade us to wash them. "Go, go outside and have fun with your friend, Lindichkeh."

After introducing Lori to the kids who were at the park that night, we stayed until nearly ten. During our walk home, Lori said, "Your friends were so nice to me, and they don't even know me. I doubt if my friends would be as nice to anyone they didn't know. And yours are all so down-to-earth, too. You're lucky."

"What do you mean, 'down-to-earth'?" I asked.

"They're not stuck up like some kids are."

"They all liked you. I think Mike thought you were really pretty. He wanted to be the only guy to help push your swing. That's what boys do around here when they like a girl."

"When they like you, they push your swing? I've never heard of that."

"Sure, that's what they always do. What do boys do in New Jersey?"

"Well, it's very different. We just go to one another's houses. You'll see when you come to visit me."

As we approached my house, we saw Father and Mother on the bench inside the tiny gated area. Mother was curled up, leaning her head against his thigh. She had seemed so good during dinner, so alive and involved. I prayed that she would remain "herself" as long as Lori was with us. I was relieved when she sat up and began talking to us.

By the time Lori had to leave on Sunday, it felt as though she had been with us for weeks and was now a member of the family. I wished that she were. It felt so good not to be the only child at home.

We all took her into the city, the two of us in the back seat, Mother and Father in front. Father even kissed Lori on the cheek when he said goodbye at the bus terminal. After she boarded the bus, he turned to me and said, "You pick very good friends, Linda. It's important in life to have nice friends."

"Friends are very important. Yes, mamaleh," Mother agreed.

No one spoke during the ride home, but for once, this quiet was a peaceful one.

CHAPTER 17
ANOTHER BREAK

About a year later, my friend Marion and I were walking home from school together. It was early November, two months after Herb left home to begin his junior year at Harvard. As we entered 2nd Street, I reached for my key, but it wasn't in its usual place.

"Uh-oh," I thought. "I hope I'm not in trouble." I opened the outside front door and the door inside the entrance hallway before reaching the one that led upstairs. I knocked several times and yelled up, "Mother, Mother!" No answer.

I went outside and again yelled up from the street, "Mo-ther!" No answer.

I wondered if she was listening to the radio so loud that she couldn't hear me. I asked Marion if I could go to her house and call Mother, hoping that she would hear the phone.

In the weeks leading up to that day, I'd known something was shifting. There were those signals, unclear, not discussed, but present. I saw differences in the way Mother looked and acted. On that day, then, when her face didn't appear at the window and she didn't respond to my calling out for her, I felt a ringing in my head and throbbing in my chest.

Once at Marion's, I called and called, but still no answer. Then I called the aunts whom Mother stayed with when she wasn't feeling well. None had seen her that day. When I called my father's office, there was no answer there, either.

It was nearing dinnertime, and I needed to go home. Marion said she'd walk with me. She asked no questions, and I offered no explanations. By the time we reached my house, the sun had set. From the street below, with the day robbed of its light, I could see only one dimly lit room in the graying light of early evening.

Only one room. My heart thumped, and I dreaded what I might find.

Marion was close behind me as I quickened my pace. I ran up the steps of the outside stoop and then pounded on our door inside. To my surprise, Dr. Andrews came down the stairs to let us in.

"What happened?" I asked, hardly able to catch my breath. "Where's my mother? Is she okay?"

"Your mother's here," Dr. Andrews said, as he patted my shoulder gently. "She got confused. She took too many pills." Marion and I followed him up the stairs as he continued talking. "I'm hoping she's going to be all right. If she's lucky, it will take a few days. But it may be as long as a week before she regains her strength."

At the top of the stairs, I saw Father and my legs weakened. He shouted for Marion to leave, and with his next breath, he shouted even louder at me, "If you had taken your key, this wouldn't have happened."

He turned and walked quickly into the bedroom. I heard the downstairs door shut as Marion left without saying a word.

I wanted to speak, but I couldn't. And I couldn't, in any way, understand how whatever happened could have been my fault.

At the door to my parents' bedroom, Dr. Andrews spoke to my father in whispered half-sentences. He had managed to pump my mother's stomach, and she wouldn't have to go to the hospital. No, there would be no police record. Their health insurance would not be affected. Yes, she would be weak and tired.

On his way out, Dr. Andrews said: "Take care of her, Linda, and start to feed her now. Feed her soft foods, anything easy to swallow, and give her lots of water. If you have a straw in the house she can drink through, that would help."

In the kitchen he packed his doctor's bag, smiled reassuringly at me, and prepared to leave. Whispering urgently, Father walked him to the top of the landing.

Dr. Andrews had said, "There will be no police record." Had my mother done something illegal? Criminals had police records. He was helping Father to cover it up so that our insurance wouldn't be affected.

I didn't have time to sort anything out, because my mother needed me. I tiptoed into her room. The blinds were shut tight and a dim bulb flickered on and off in the lamp beside the bed. What I could see of Mother's face was ghostly. The rest of her was buried in her pillow, her eyes barely open. Her body was folded up and covered up to her chin by a duvet cover and a pile of blankets.

She didn't seem to know that I was there, but, in my nervousness and confusion, I needed to talk. I wanted her to hear me, and I needed to hear my own voice. Memories returned in a rush—images and words I'd seen and heard over the years whenever Mother was sick. "I need to get rid of the demons. I need to end it all!"

Why hadn't I ever asked her what she meant? Why had I never questioned Father when he said, "Mama shouldn't be home alone today," or when he told me to have my key on me at all times? Why hadn't I asked about the treatments Mama got when we had to take her "to calm her nerves" and I was told to bring a friend? I couldn't remember ever being told not to ask. Had it been an unspoken rule, a part of the fabric of our family, the secret code that came with being born "the girl"?

Did my mother's sickness, which Herb didn't have the courage to tell me about, cause this new crisis? The more I thought about it, the more sense it made, and the more sense it made, the more I needed to scold and lecture someone. Words began to tumble out of my mouth.

"It's a sin for anyone to do what you did," I said, addressing Mother's collapsed body. "That's what doctors are for. They're supposed to tell you how much medicine to take and when to take it.

You can't decide that yourself. Only God can decide who will live and who will die."

I didn't know where my words came from. The Bible? Or was I making it all up in an effort to kill the silence, to protect myself by turning on her, making her the culprit and not the victim?

Even though I knew she couldn't hear me, her silence only compelled me to talk more. "Life's a precious gift. You must never do this again. Do you hear me? I'm your daughter, Linda. Do you hear what I'm saying?"

No answer.

Now I began asking myself questions. How important was it to be good or kind? Those qualities hadn't prevented Mother from becoming sick. If there was a God, He hadn't rewarded her goodness. If the mind itself is such a God-given gift, why had God decided to twist Mother's, to torture her and, in turn, all of us?

I ran to our refrigerator, took out some applesauce, put it in a cup, and grabbed a teaspoon from the drawer. I held my mother's chin in my hand and began to feed her, slowly and carefully.

"Please try to eat. Dr. Andrews said you have to eat."

After she took a drop of the sauce into her mouth, I ran back into the kitchen, filled a glass with water and found one of our summer plastic straws to help her sip. Applesauce, water, applesauce, water. I did my best to follow Dr. Andrews's instructions.

I felt trapped inside the small space of her bedroom, seeing only her helpless body. I remembered how she used to hold my chin in her hand as she fed me when I was a baby. In that moment, our roles were reversed. In the act of talking and feeding, I crossed over into another way of knowing.

I told myself it was all right not to feel guilty for not having my key. I even convinced myself I wasn't to blame, that I wasn't the problem. Yet as I spooned the applesauce into Mother's dry mouth, all I could think about were the stories she told me about her childhood, about immigrating to America without parents, having to learn a new language, new customs, and always being uprooted. I remembered what she had said about having been sent to live with one family and then another and never having felt loved or wanted. I kept seeing my poor mother as a victim who, as a grown woman, had not outgrown her victimhood.

I never called Herb, although he had asked me to, because I believed it was my duty to cope with whatever happened. Now, in his absence, there was no escape. Mother was screaming for attention in the one way she knew. I could now piece together what Dr. Andrews had implied: she had reached for every pill bottle in sight, swallowing as many pills as she could until she passed out.

I pitied the sight of her, but I hated what she had done to herself and felt anguished, abandoned. The pills. The key. Not having the key. Father. Dr. Andrews. The police. The insurance. Applesauce. My mind raced. I couldn't hold onto a single thought before the next, even more threatening one appeared. I refilled the bowl because I needed to give her more applesauce. As she painfully began to swallow as much as would fit on the tip of her tongue, I looked at her and mourned the loss of the mother I believed I would no longer have.

I didn't realize Father was in the room until he said, "Go fix yourself some dinner. It's time you should have something to eat. I'll sit here with Mama."

I went into the kitchen, but food was the furthest thought from my mind. I stood there unable to move, and then returned to the bedroom where Father sat with his head in his hands, staring at Mother.

I stayed in the doorway, my hand on the doorknob. "I think I have to go to sleep," I said.

"Now? It's still early," he said. He looked so old.

"I'm very tired."

"Sure, Linda. Rest. Go." He folded his hands in his lap.

I never changed into pajamas that night. Staying in my clothing felt safer. Afraid even of the darkness, I called out to Father, "Please leave on the bathroom light."

I heard him walk down the hall, but he didn't say a word to me. As he walked back into their bedroom, I pictured him sitting on the chair next to Mother who, still limp, lay in bed with those blankets up to her chin.

I was afraid for Mother, afraid for myself, and afraid of all the thoughts entering my mind. It didn't matter that Father was just down the hall. Mother had been rescued from Death's door, and my brother was hundreds of miles away.

Terrified, with nowhere to turn but toward the cold wall, I folded my arms across my chest and held onto myself as tightly as I could until sleep came. At last, the day was over.

In the weeks that followed, no one thought it necessary to talk with me about Mother and what was now clearly our family's secret. Nobody asked me what I understood, what I needed. Foolishly, they must have believed I'd been in this world before, that I didn't have to be asked or told anything.

Yet, as a twelve-year-old, I understood little, if anything, about Mother's illness and didn't have words to describe her state of mind or her condition. All I knew was that I had no control over it and no choice—I had to deal with it. The weight of its burden was heavier than ever.

I was also at war with myself. The part that loved my mother was in conflict with the part that was repulsed by her inability to defend herself from her demons. I walked toward the mirror above her bureau, looked long and hard at myself, and told the person I saw there that whatever happened in life, I would never lose my self-control. I would never surrender and become a victim.

From that time on, I trusted in my intellect. I refused to acknowledge sadness, anxiety, or loneliness, and never spoke about anything personal. I walked with my head high and was determined never to appear vulnerable.

Although I continued to protect our family's secret and succeeded in fooling others most of the time, I could no longer protect myself from my thoughts or from the reverberations of mother's recurring illness. No matter how hard I fought to suppress it, I realized that it had become my shadow companion. Wherever I went, it followed me, reminding me that I was different from everyone I knew.

CHAPTER 18
MOTHERS AND MADNESS

Months passed, and the following summer was a good one. I was thirteen. Mother wasn't having any of her "spells," and I had fun at the beach with my friends in the neighborhood.

I hadn't realized how much I missed Saturdays at the Workshop until I returned to acting classes in the fall. Then I understood what Herb had said about making new friends. During one of our lunches at Whelan's Drug Store, Lori invited me for a sleepover at her house in New Jersey. When my parents gave me permission to go, Father said: "Just be a lady. Be polite, like Lori. Use your good manners."

The Saturday we went to her house was gloriously warm. New Yorkers, as well as tourists, packed the streets of Manhattan, and the city's energy was contagious. After class, we raced to change from our leotards and tights into our street clothes, but instead of walking to the Port Authority Terminal, as I had expected, Lori insisted that we take a taxi.

"I'll pay," she said, noticing my bewildered expression. "It's okay. Don't worry."

After we got out of the cab at the bus terminal, I paid for my ticket with money Father had given me. We boarded a luxurious bus and found seats next to each other.

"I've never been on a bus where seats have such soft cushions," I said delightedly. "This is really fancy."

"It's the only kind of bus I know," she said. "Someone always drives me where I need to go, or I take a cab."

As the bus started its route out from the city, I started to feel queasy. It was similar to the Sundays when we visited Aunt Pauley or Tanteh. But, why now, I wondered, when I should be excited and happy? When I thought about it, I realized that the queasiness began when a picture of Lori's mother popped into my head. It was the same uneasiness I'd felt whenever I'd seen her pick up Lori after class.

Unlike any of the mothers I knew in Brighton, her hair was bleached blonde and perfectly coiffed. She wore silk dresses and spiked-heeled shoes in colors other than black. She had the kind of glamour that simply didn't exist in Brighton. I only saw such women in the movies.

Yet it wasn't simply her hair or her elegant clothing that was off-putting. It was the way she stared at me and the other kids, never looking directly at us. She'd simply say a quick hello, nothing more. We all felt uncomfortable, but none of us told Lori. We didn't think that was what friends should do.

When the bus driver announced that her stop would be next, Lori and I grabbed our hatboxes from above our seats. I followed her from the bus through a small terminal.

"We're smack in the middle of Main Street," Lori said, while waving to a taxi driver. "Come, that man over there is waiting for us," she said, pointing to someone in front of the terminal's entrance. "My mom called in advance. He'll be taking us home."

The cab driver drove us through a quaint village, with Lori pointing to various landmarks: the public library, her favorite book store, the dance studio where her sister studied, and then the high school. "That's the public high school," she said. "I won't be going there. My private school goes through 12th grade."

"I didn't know you go to private school. How many kids are in your class?" I asked. "My class has twenty-three kids."

"We have nine girls in my eighth-grade class. It's small, like our class at the Workshop."

"I forgot you're in eighth grade," I said, instantly feeling very young and very different.

The cab rode through the center of town and climbed a steep hill where beautiful homes appeared on both sides of the street. The driver made a sharp turn into a small cul-de-sac, where a gray-shingled house with white shutters and a yellow Dutch door stood high up on a hill. A perfectly manicured lawn stretched from the bottom of the hill to the top, where the house was majestically perched.

"That's your house?" I managed to ask.

The path to the front door had a rock garden on one side and a few steep steps leading to a porch. Lori had no need to use a key or ring the bell, as a woman immediately opened the door for us. Until that moment, I thought it was only in the movies that people actually had black servants—women who wore white ruffled aprons over short-sleeved dresses, just like the maid in *Gone with the Wind*. Yet standing right in front of me, taking our bags from our hands, was Betty, who Lori said lived in her house, cleaned, cooked, and served her family their meals.

We entered through the yellow door into a large flagstone foyer. A beautiful antique mirror with sconces on either side covered most of one wall. A large tropical fish aquarium built into the wall on the opposite side called to mind the tiny fishbowl I had thrown away when my one and only goldfish had died.

As we stepped down into a large, breathtaking living room, I could see the skyline of New York City through a bay window. Lori pointed to the other side of the room, where a huge baby grand piano stood regally, polished to perfection.

"Sometimes, when I'm doing my homework in my room, I hear my mother playing," she said. "In the evenings we sing folk songs and Gilbert and Sullivan operettas."

Who was Gilbert? And Sullivan? All of this was foreign to me.

She then walked me through the house, pointing out various pieces of furniture, telling me her family went antiquing on weekends. My shoes sank into thick, plush carpeting as we walked down the hallway toward the bedrooms. She invited me to peek inside her parents' room, where everything was in soft colors of dusty pink and pale gray. "All the bedrooms have built-in drawers in the wall so that space isn't taken up by dressers," Lori informed me, as we reached her bedroom, which had two beds and two sinks. A pocket door closed off her room and her sister's from the rest of the house, and a bathroom separated their two rooms.

The maid had left our bags inside Lori's room. She told me to put mine in front of one of the two beds. Then we washed our hands and got ready for dinner. I saw her parents for the first time as we stepped into the dining room. They were seated at the large table, already set with fine china and fancy stemware.

I was beginning to think the entire house was a movie set, a fairytale, make-believe world I might never again be inside. I paid attention to every detail so that I'd never forget any of it.

Lori invited me to sit next to her at the table, and her younger sister, Karen, sat opposite us. She remained quiet, though she flashed sweet smiles my way every once in a while. The only comment to me was from Lori's father, who said, "I understand you're from Brooklyn. Have you always lived there?"

"Yes," I answered, too intimidated to say more.

I wasn't spoken to again for the rest of the meal, but I felt Lori's mother's constant stare. Each time she looked my way, I lowered my head, not wishing to face her frightening, unwelcoming expression.

When Betty served dessert, a plate filled with all sorts of delicious cookies placed inside a circle of fresh, red strawberries, Lori's parents started to talk about politics. By that time, my head was aching. Though it was difficult to pay attention, I realized they were talking about their local Republican ticket and a friend, "Dave," who was running for Congress.

"Those Democrats," her father said derisively. "They'd give everything away for a vote. Why anyone supports the Democratic ticket is beyond me!"

I couldn't wait to leave the table and was thrilled when Lori asked if we could be excused. I waited until we were alone in her bedroom, with the door shut, before confronting her.

"I thought you told me you were Jewish," I said. "Why did you lie?"

"What are you talking about?" she asked, looking confused.

"Everyone knows that if someone's Jewish they vote for Democrats. And from the way your father spoke, he's definitely a Republican. So, you can't be Jewish."

"Of course we're Jewish," she said, laughing. With a sympathetic smile and the look of a caring older sister, she added, "We're Jewish on both sides of my family. But I told you my father's a lawyer."

"What does that have to do with anything?"

"I don't know, but he says the Republicans do a better job protecting what he cares about."

"I still can't believe it. I was so sure that all Jews were Democrats. Maybe all those who aren't are lawyers?"

Saying that made her laugh again. Then I laughed, too. We laughed deep belly laughs for at least five minutes. By then, it was eleven o'clock, the time her parents said we should go to sleep. Lori turned off an overhead light and left on a dimly lit table lamp.

Feeling tired but more at ease, I began to snuggle into the warmth of a down comforter, stroking the silky sheet and pillowcase beneath me, wanting to tuck them into my memory.

I assumed we were going to sleep, but Lori sat up, leaning against the wall behind her. "I want to tell you something, Linda. I don't want to scare you, but I want you to know about my mother. I don't want you to think she's mean because she's not warm and friendly like your mother."

I knew then that she had seen me avoiding her mother. As I watched Lori twist one of the cuffs of her pajama sleeves, I sensed she wanted to tell me something more. When she turned toward me, she said, "My mother gets sick from time to time. And when she's sick, she's weird. Sometimes she runs into the street shouting words that nobody understands. My father has to run after her and bring her back. Other times he takes her to the hospital."

I was stunned. My cheeks felt hot, and as she stared at me, I wondered if she had any idea about what I was thinking. She asked, "Are you okay?"

How could I tell her it felt as though she'd been inside my head, telling me things about my own mother, even though she was talking about hers? I answered, "God, Lori, I think my mother gets sick in the same way."

"I doubt it," she said, without hesitation.

"Well, I remember one time when my mother ran out of our house in her nightgown. I couldn't understand anything she said. My father had to catch her before she ran into traffic."

"I can't believe it. Your mother seemed so different when I met her." Then, after a long, reflective pause, she added, "I suppose I did think she had sad eyes, but I never thought it was from this." After pausing again, she asked, "Does your mother get those terrible treatments?"

"I know she gets treatments, but I don't know what kind."

"When she comes out, does she look like her eyes are half-closed and she doesn't know where she is?"

"Kind of."

Now there was no stopping Lori. "They're called shock treatments," she said. "I read about them in one of my father's books."

Her words were the same ones I'd heard Father use to describe the treatments my mother received. Lori needed to know everything, when I needed not to know. She asked questions and read books, while I told myself not to think about what was happening.

That night in New Jersey, facing each other, on beds three feet apart, I listened for the first time to the horrifying details of Mother's treatments. Determined to share it all with me, Lori began, "People have their arms and legs strapped to a table."

Squeezing my eyes shut, I told her I didn't think I could hear any more. She continued anyway. "Something is placed in their mouths so they don't bite their tongues. Then they're shocked with electrical currents."

"Oh, God."

"But you have to know what happens, Lin, if that's what they do to your mother."

I wanted to throw up. Terrifying images of what she must have endured raced through my mind, and I felt dizzy thinking about it. I even began to question whether I was making up a past that never existed or whether the dark days, the terrible times in my family, really had happened.

The only comfort I felt came from knowing that I now had a friend whose mother, though different from mine in so many ways, seemed to suffer just as mine did.

"Nobody tells me what's happening," I said, tears rolling down my cheeks. "So I force myself not to think about it. Aren't you ever scared?"

"Sure, but I have to take care of my sister. She starts to shake and asks me if our mother's going to die. I tell her that she's not, but I don't know."

"You're scared, too, aren't you?"

"I just get angrier. I wish she'd break a leg, something easy to see and easy to fix."

"Angry? Don't you think that's mean?"

Lori said nothing. The cozy feeling I'd felt when we were laughing only moments earlier had disappeared, and her room now felt as unsafe as the rest of her house. Yet I still felt compelled to tell her more. "My mother was sick after my brother's Bar Mitzvah," I continued. "And she was sick again after he left home to go to Harvard. She told me how sad she felt about not having parents who could share special occasions with her. I just pray that it won't happen again."

"I stopped praying a long time ago. I know it'll happen again. My mother goes nuts. My father gets angry. My sister shakes."

I asked hesitantly, "Do any of your friends know about your mother?"

"Maybe from their parents, but I don't talk about it with anyone but my friend Jon. He has a brother who's sick. We sort of understand each other."

"None of my friends or their parents knows anything," I said, suddenly wondering if that was true. "You're the first person in the whole world I've ever talked to about this."

Then I realized how exhausting talking had been. I got back underneath the comforter and saw Lori do the same. For one brief moment, we smiled at one another, mirroring a sense of relief and reassurance at having found someone with whom we could share stories of mothers. Mothers and madness, and Lori and me.

CHAPTER 19
THE AUDITION

With the encouragement of my teachers at the Dramatic Workshop, I auditioned for the High School of Performing Arts. Unfortunately, they didn't tell me what to expect for my audition, assuming, I guess, that it was my family's responsibility—and I was, therefore, totally unprepared. Neither Mother nor Father knew anything about how to select a monologue and even less about how I should explain why I wanted to attend the prestigious school.

During one of Herb's weekly calls home from Harvard, I asked him for help. He selected a monologue from *Our Town*, by Thornton Wilder. Since I was close in age to the girl whose role I would play, he assumed I would understand her, adding, "I just know you can do this one."

I received the monologue in the mail, typed perfectly on his college stationery, but we never discussed how I should perform it. I simply memorized the words, rehearsed them alone, and remained blissfully hopeful, until, the week before the audition, when Mother began to slip into one of her states.

Once again, I became fearful about going to sleep at night, anticipating being awakened by her pacing, her chatter, and her early morning arguments with Father. I also knew that her decline meant I'd be going to the audition alone.

The night before the audition, I set my hair for the occasion and slept in twenty-four pink foam hair rollers, the kind with the plastic clips. But in the morning, when I took out the rollers, my heart sank. I hated what I saw in the mirror. Either I had set my hair too tightly or I'd slept fitfully, because my hair looked much too short, the curls much too tight. I looked anything but stylish.

Because I wasn't sure how to dress for the occasion, I tried to imagine what clothes Mother would have helped me choose. I tried on various combinations of tops and skirts, and eventually selected a pale pink sweater, a white leather collar through which I slipped a scarf, a gray poodle skirt with white bobby socks, and black and white saddle shoes. I didn't wear makeup, but I did dab on some of Mother's red lipstick, assuring myself that how I looked wasn't that important.

I then took what seemed to be an endless subway ride into Manhattan, starting with the train getting stuck between the first two stations. When it reached my stop, I walked north instead of south, east instead of west, and then had to backtrack to locate the old building that then housed the High School of Performing Arts.

A student posted at the front door asked to see the card I'd been sent with my name and number printed on it. I handed it to her, and she responded in an affected, intimidating voice, "Go downstairs to the cafeteria and wait with the others until your number is called."

In that huge cafeteria, I began to tremble. Everywhere, I saw the presence of mothers and felt the absence of mine. Mothers were putting makeup on daughters, straightening the shirt collars and ties of their sons. I immediately rationalized that whoever auditioned us would notice how mature I was, having come unescorted. The others, with their mothers in attendance, would surely be viewed as far less mature, not capable of coming on their own.

When my name was called and I went upstairs alone, no one knew if I'd been escorted or not. Worse still, I was the only girl wearing bobby socks and saddle shoes. All the others wore nylon stockings and adult-looking pumps.

The audition was in an upstairs classroom, where a panel of three teachers sat behind a long desk. Before I even began my monologue, they asked me to face them and shot one question after another my way: What was my name? How did I spell it? Where did I live and had I always lived there? How would I describe myself academically and what was my reason for wanting to study at their school? All the while I could feel their eyes scrutinizing every part of me—not just my face and body but how I spoke. It seemed clear that they were trying to figure out if I would be an asset to their school.

I was called back for a second audition three weeks later. By then, however, Mother was in the throes of a full-blown episode. Every night my sleep was interrupted by her talking aloud in words I didn't understand, even when they were in English. She'd pace nervously from room to room, never even noticing me in the morning.

I did my best to ignore her, hoping that her illness would magically disappear, but when she began wringing her hands and calling out, "Mama, Mama, where are you?" I knew she would only deteriorate further. She'd continually repeat those words, making mornings the most terrifying part of each day.

Father was busy scheduling her treatments and arranging for her to stay with one of my aunts. Herb was at Harvard, and no one was available for me. So, I did what I had to do. I went to school, did my eighth-grade homework, got all A's, and while I was out of the house, I forced myself not to think about the sounds and sights of my mother's incoherence.

Whenever thoughts about Mother crept into my mind and I'd remember the day she took pills and almost died, I'd twirl my hair and grow sick to my stomach. So I tried to cut myself off from frightening images of Mother, and especially the jumbled sounds of her talking to dead people.

To distract myself, I'd spend time with my friends and my schoolwork. Volunteering to be a class monitor to aid teachers was also helpful, keeping my focus on other people, not on myself and not on Mother.

By evening, I'd take comfort in seeing her rest on the sofa, watching TV. If it was Tuesday, she'd laugh with Milton Berle. "Uncle Miltie," though not prescribed, was her best therapy. I reveled in hearing her laugh, and whatever hope I could conjure up rode on the crest of each little giggle that Uncle Miltie was somehow able to evoke.

But then, when she would again be unable to sleep, my anxiety returned, intensified. Nothing really had changed.

Three weeks later, at my second audition, the stress at home collided with the excitement of the day. I was painfully unable to concentrate. Mother's agonized face and disheveled appearance were foremost in my thoughts. As other girls put mascara on their eyelashes and boys slicked back their hair, their excitement—in sharp contrast with how I was feeling—only exaggerated my emptiness.

Once inside the audition room, I barely heard the questions I was asked. Instead, the words that echoed inside my head were Mother's when she called out, "Mama, Mama, help me."

When I was told to improvise a scene of calling a friend on the telephone, I apparently paid no attention to how many times my finger moved around the face of an imaginary phone. When asked if I knew that every phone number had seven digits, I realized that I had done something very wrong. Since nothing was registering properly, though, I could only offer an awkward response.

I don't remember what I wore for that second audition, and I recall little else about the day. I only remember thinking it made no difference what school I attended or whether strangers thought I was talented when my mother didn't know who I was.

What did any of it matter, when the world into which I'd been thrust was noisy, bleak, and overwhelming? What difference did it make when adults looked at me and didn't really see me?

Weeks later, during a Wednesday morning assembly program, I was summoned from the auditorium by Mr. Meisel, my eighth-grade English teacher. He took me aside and told me he'd just received a call saying I hadn't been accepted to the High School of Performing Arts. He expressed his sympathy, but by then I was no longer listening. I thanked him politely for informing me and tried to sound nonchalant, as though it didn't really matter—but, of course, it mattered terribly.

I knew I hadn't been accepted because I hadn't done my best, and I hadn't done my best because Mother's illness had shrouded that day, robbing me of my ability to be myself, to think clearly, to perform well. I knew that I had been denied the thrill of pursuing a dream, and to protect myself, I now had to put that dream to rest. It didn't even occur to me that I had a right to feel angry. Not then.

Unable to talk to anyone about our family's secret, I pushed down all the feelings that might have surfaced and pretended that what had mattered so much to me was unimportant. Once again I found myself minimizing another disappointment and sense of failure. I looked in the mirror and rehearsed what I'd say to my friends. "I'd rather go to the local high school where I'll be with all of you. I don't want to travel on subways for two hours a day, anyway."

I must have sounded convincing because no one challenged me when I told them. They bought the lie, and I secretly approved of my performance. I was able to act, after all.

CHAPTER 20
I WON'T BE LIKE MOTHER

"**T**hose need to be placed into a bra, dear," the woman in Mother's corset shop said with a patronizing smile, her gaze alternating between my eyes and my breasts. Along with all the other girls I knew, I was unprepared at the age of twelve for the changes occurring inside my body and my brain. It was of little comfort knowing that my friends all were moving through adolescence as clumsily as I was, acting immaturely one moment and grown-up the next.

For me, the turmoil of my teenage years was compounded by constant anxiety. Fiercely determined to maintain my silence about Mother's illness and to enjoy the hours I spent in school, I was torn between loyalty to my mother and an urgent need to be like my friends and to spend time with them. I couldn't feel carefree and silly as I perceived so many of my friends to be.

I was similar to them in that we all seemed to experience everything as black or white, good or bad, all or nothing. But there was another, more subtle difference, one that kept me separate and alone. We were all moody, yet whenever my moods shifted, and especially when I started to develop physically into a young woman, I couldn't stop myself from identifying with Mother. Despite my promise to myself never to be like her, any uncomfortable feeling frightened me, making me wonder if I could keep that promise. I longed for someone to reassure me that I was okay, and that I would remain okay. But without sharing my secret, how could I gain reassurance from anyone? And whom could I trust?

I was convinced that none of my friends feared what I feared: hospitalization or becoming a burden to my family. I assumed my peers worried about the normal concerns described in *Seventeen* magazine: having acne, being popular, winning and losing friends, and preparing to get into a good college. Then, too, my friends were constantly disappointing me. My status within the group changed as girls I'd known all my life were becoming as unpredictable as the boys they talked about incessantly. They broke off into cliques, adding and dropping members as frequently as changes in the weather. Nothing they did or said made sense to me. I just couldn't count on anything to remain the same, and that left me feeling even more insecure.

Old friends still talked to me during school hours, especially when they needed my help with assignments, but I was excluded from after school get-togethers. My phone rarely rang, and when I dared to confront anyone, I was told that I took everything too seriously. A neat euphemism, I thought, for saying I was imagining it all. In the back of my mind, I heard an echo of Mrs. Kellert saying I was "too serious for a little girl."

While figuring out how to tolerate the immature behavior of my peers, I eventually maneuvered my way back into the group, though I never believed that my position would ever again be solid.

I trusted none of them as I had before, and I never again felt free to be totally myself. Without anyone to share close conversations, I lost my footing.

Instead, I felt that my life was totally unmanageable—an overriding belief that I was becoming more and more like Mother.

My need for boys to find me attractive seemed greater than that of any of the girls I knew. That was probably because Herb got married when I was fourteen. Spending time with him and my sister-in-law, Dee, when they were openly affectionate and very much in love, made me feel lonelier still, distorting my sense of what was appropriate for someone my age.

Also, unlike other girls who enjoyed fooling around with boys in the balcony of a movie theater or at the beach at sunset, I mistook such "fun" for expressions of love. I was too intense to see them for what they were: typical adolescent behavior. Instead, I interpreted any interest from a boy as meaning much more than he intended. Of course, this led to a series of disappointments, and I could never understand how a boy could be affectionate one day and pretend not to know me the next.

I didn't know how to voice my needs or ask to be treated differently. I'd never seen any woman do these things well—not even my new sister-in-law, Dee, who was passive and undemanding with my brother, though assertive and open when we were alone.

I hated being at the mercy of anyone's whims, and I wasn't carefree enough to enjoy the game-playing that I saw other girls my age engaging in with delight. As I saw it, guys sat in the control booth, and I wanted more than anything to know how that felt.

While acting flirtatious came easily to many of my friends, it felt unnatural to me. Whenever I pretended as if I knew how to be coquettish, I actually felt manipulative and stupid. Then, when the boys I liked seemed to give other girls their affection, I naturally concluded I couldn't be both feminine and intelligent. At least not with the boys I knew.

So I decided that acting smart was preferable to acting sexy. It was safer keeping my distance, behaving in ways that felt comfortable. I philosophized about art, literature, and the theater. I was not about to become someone's girlfriend, risk being rejected, and feel—as my father had made me feel—unimportant.

Because I was a good listener, guys began calling again. However, they invariably asked me how they could get some other girl to like them. That was proof enough that I was seen from the neck up, a talking head that was even better on the phone than in person. Once again, I was invisible. If I didn't count as far as any boy was concerned, then was he my enemy? If so, how could I protect myself?

I never forgot the fact that Mother referred to Father as her enemy. It didn't matter that she did so during the times when she was sick. Her words stuck in my mind, making it impossible for me to express my true feelings when I was with boys. Instead, I kept the focus on what I thought were the necessities: succeeding in my classes, appearing happy, and covering my pimples with Acnomel.

Summers gave me reprieve, as they had when I was younger. To earn money, I lied about my age from the time I was fifteen, leaving home to be a counselor at sleep-away camps. I was hired to be a senior counselor to junior counselors who were actually older than me. During the days, I performed my job with authority. In the evenings and on days off, I found romance, as did everyone. I enjoyed flings that felt like love in the heat of July, in the romantic setting of bunk life and bonfires.

It was easier during those summers away from home to act in more normal, carefree ways. It didn't matter that I seldom knew very much about my summer boyfriend. He was the lifeguard or the folk singer who lived in the Bronx or in Queens, a year or two older than I was and always a good student.

The rituals were the same. On days off, we'd hitchhike into town. On nights off, we'd kiss under the stars after the campers were asleep. Our times together were innocent enough and intimate enough to mask my loneliness.

Yet back home during the cool nights of September, when the mailbox was empty, when letters stopped coming and there were no phone calls, I again felt abandoned.

Despite academic achievements and extracurricular activities, my social life during the school year had the appearance of being busy and the reality of feeling empty. My male friends in high school continued to remain intellectual buddies, either because I gave them all the wrong signals or because I totally misread theirs.

After being dumped by my summer boyfriends, I began to believe that relationships with guys and love itself would never be constant, could never be trusted. To win my affection, guys would say what they knew I wanted to hear but would then disappear, reinforcing my feelings that I was not someone who deserved to be treated with respect.

Father suffered his first heart attack in 1957. He was fifty-six, and I was sixteen. He was never hospitalized, because his fear of hospitals was greater than his fear of dying. Along with Dr. Andrews, who made daily house calls, Mother waited on him day and night, nursing him back to health. Fortunately, at this time she was doing much better.

Within a few months, pale and shaky, Father was back on his feet and back at work. During the next ten years, he suffered two more attacks but still continued to work.

Since so much of life at home was out of my control, the new obstacles of these years—teenage boys at the mercy of their hormones—inflamed my anxiety. Without warning, I'd experience an uneasiness in the pit of my stomach or a heaviness in my chest, instead of what I yearned for: a sense of comfort and appreciation.

Until now, it had been Mother's illness that had made the ground beneath me shake. Now, as I became an adolescent, the upheavals were my own.

CHAPTER 21
FIRST LOVE

Perhaps to make me consider living at home during college, Mother and Father decided to move when I was a senior in high school. Our new apartment was on Corbin Place, in Manhattan Beach, a notch up on the economic ladder, in a two-family house with a porch facing the ocean.

Fortunately, Mother handled the stress of packing and moving well. She remained fairly stable throughout the year, allowing me to keep my focus on my studies and apply to college. At school, I continued to succeed academically. I was invited to join the principal's Great Books Club and served as editor-in-chief of our high school's senior yearbook.

Mother and Father protested when I applied to an out-of-town college, and Mother said, "Why go far away when Brooklyn College is such a good school? You could live at home and have my home-cooked meals." But Herb had paved the way for me, taking the sting out of Mother's attempt to keep me at home.

I realized that my leaving might be yet another loss for Mother, but I couldn't let that deter me. To her credit, she tried to conceal whatever sadness she may have felt. She even sounded proud when an acceptance letter arrived from Bennington College, the school of my choice, along with a scholarship offer.

Father's reaction was more surprising. The day the letter arrived, I stuck my head out the window and shouted the news to him as he was parking the car. He looked up at me, as though caught dead in his tracks, stunned, speechless. His simple expectations for the girl in the family didn't come close to what had just happened. A curious expression came over his face as he came up the stairs and sat at the kitchen table. "A scholarship, Linda? They gave you a scholarship?" It was as if he were trying to figure me out, to find out who I was. I smiled at him lovingly, waiting for a response. He shrugged. That was it.

While my friends were delighted to leave home for college, if only to be free of their parents, I was ambivalent about giving up my efforts to protect Mother. Excited as I was to be attending a women's college in bucolic New England, I still left feeling guilty and fearful of the price I might pay for leaving.

Although some friends had already been sexually active and others talked about wanting to be, my focus, when not worrying about Mother's state of mind, was on school work. My safety net.

Classes at Bennington gave me the chance to grow intellectually, but weekends always presented a problem. When young men from neighboring colleges arrived to check out the scene and "look over the new crop," it always made me uncomfortable. I never understood why other girls thought this way of meeting guys was fun. I never felt carefree enough to simply enjoy it. I dated occasionally and attended a few fraternity parties, but being around people my age who were drinking and making small talk felt demeaning. Each time I left, I had a sinking feeling that I was an outsider with little hope of ever fitting in.

Around this time, though, Mother started to get help from new anti-depressive and anti-psychotic medications, and I felt freer to open up new ways of being in the world. My social life, too, began to change my junior year, when I found myself drawn to Dan, one of the few male graduate students on campus, who had been accepted into the college's privileged dance, theater, and art programs. Dan was a non-practicing Christian, and I was a semi-practicing Jew. He was the youngest of five siblings and had grown up in a rather affluent family. Both of his parents were college-educated, and he had been exposed to a cultural life that I hadn't known existed when I was growing up.

But during long walks in the lush countryside of our Vermont campus, we found ourselves talking easily and endlessly, and soon discovered that our different upbringings were far less important than what we shared: a love of nature, the arts, and literature.

While my teachers were opening my mind to a world outside the one I knew in Brighton, Dan was exposing me to a new way of experiencing life—a contemplative way of moving through each day. Whenever I watched him choreograph a dance, or when we explored Bennington's back roads and hidden treasures in pre-World War II cemeteries, or picked wildflowers and arranged them into mini bouquets of art, I began to experience new feelings awakening inside me, feelings that seemed to have long been neglected.

Midway through the semester, a medical student I had dated in New York the previous summer called at the last minute to say he wouldn't be coming up for a weekend we had planned. Since I had told my friends about his upcoming visit, I tried to hide my anger and disappointment when I shared the news at dinner. Sensing my mood as we left the dining hall, Dan asked if he could walk back to my house with me.

I wanted company and invited him into my room. Knowing that he had planned to work on a paper in the library, I offered my desk, but he chose the floor, leaning against the wall with a textbook and notebook on his lap. I sat on the bed planning to translate passages from Proust's *Swann's Way*.

As we went through the motions of doing something ordinary, we grew intensely aware of each other's presence in the shared stillness.

At that point, I stopped writing and Dan, staring out the window, whispered: "Lin needs someone to love and somebody to love her."

As he spoke of me in the third person, I thought he saw me as a girl who had been stood up, a girl who was lonely and needy.

"You know," I said, unable to stop the tears from rolling down my cheeks, "that guy who called tonight, he's not someone I care about. He's probably every Jewish mother's dream for a daughter because he's going to be a doctor. The truth is he thinks he's God's gift to the universe. If he ever calls again, though, I'm never going out with him."

Dan stood, gathered his things, reached over to my bookcase where I had a box of tissues, handed me one, and said softly, "Would you like to walk to the Rain Barrel?"

That New England night was balmy and beautiful. The stars seemed an arm's length away when we walked to the French café at the edge of campus. There, in the romantic setting of a dimly lit room, candles flickering in tiny glass cups, he looked directly into my eyes, reached his hand across the table, and for the first time, put his outstretched hand into mine. As the candle allowed me to see his deep, dark eyes, he smiled at me. Unable to speak, I hesitantly returned his smile and felt more protected, more cared for than ever. I don't remember the taste of the peach melbas we ordered, but I vividly recall the shiver that passed through me. After that night, we spent even more time together, parting ways a few weeks later, when the college's ten-week break took him to California and me home to Brighton.

When we returned to campus in March, we were nearly inseparable. He tried to dissuade me from falling in love with him, saying, "I'd never want to hurt you." But I ignored his warnings. I did my best to reassure him, saying, "I'm a big person. I can take care of myself."

It was easy to get caught up in romance at twenty, and though I had learned that anything good never seemed to last, I pushed on. With the exuberance that love breeds, I had more energy than ever before. When we stayed out late and I had an early-morning class the next day, I was wide awake and fully prepared. Yet I was splitting myself into two people. As long as I was in Vermont, I continued to turn away from my Brighton self and my family. I was accountable only to the Vermont me. Even when I called home each week, I never spoke about Dan. I was far enough away to believe I was actually another person living another life, a separate life that had nothing to do with my parents, or being Jewish, or the complications our relationship might present.

After all, I *had* grown up in a Jewish ghetto. I had gone to Hebrew School. I knew about pogroms and Hitler and had been told how important it was to the Jewish community for Jews to marry Jews. There was a very real part of my brain that knew that I should be with someone Jewish, but I put that part aside. I was in love, and having waited so long to experience the thrill and release of being in a relationship with a creative and intellectual partner, it was too special to give up.

Summer vacation left us on different coasts again—Dan in California, me living at home and working in Manhattan. Again, our relationship had a reprieve. We remained in touch through phone calls and letters, and I dated no one, holding tight to the belief that we were a couple.

When I returned in the fall for my senior year, it wasn't long before I sensed something had changed. At first, the difference was so subtle, I once again questioned whether I was imagining something that didn't exist. Although Dan said nothing to make me believe his feelings had changed, I'd notice the features of his face tighten, the sweetness in his eyes turn pensive without warning or reason. When we were alone, he remained kind and thoughtful. Yet in social situations, he walked away, talked with others, and danced with girls I knew he didn't like. Worst of all, he didn't seem to care about how hurt I was that he didn't acknowledge our relationship in public.

He was detached and aloof one day, warm and loving the next, and none of it made any sense. Previously, he never hesitated to share stories about his family or his friends, but now he grew secretive about his life away from college, refusing to talk about the many letters he received from friends on the West Coast. When I asked who they were, he seemed annoyed and never really answered my questions. Instead, he alluded to having known them from school, from friends of the family, from friends of friends. "No one important," he'd say.

I knew I was on shaky ground when I felt elated and hopeful one minute, frightened and abandoned the next. Such perilously familiar feelings began to push buttons that terrified me. However, I had learned to tolerate unpredictable behavior—it was, after all, what I knew how to do. So I remained loyal to Dan. Instead of ending the relationship, I waited passively for something to change or for Dan to tell me what was really going on. But he didn't, so the awkwardness between us grew, and I knew that things couldn't continue as they were.

I turned to Anne, a friend who had been close to many of the graduate students, hoping she could explain Dan's behavior. We walked along one of the campus's country roads, slender white birch trees arching gracefully on either side, until we reached the music rehearsal rooms in Jennings Hall. I felt particularly at peace after listening to Anne practice a Beethoven sonata and decided that was the moment to confide in her.

It took only a few seconds for her to reply. "I don't think Dan's as committed to you as you may think he is, Lin."

"What do you mean?"

"Well, most of the guys here see themselves as free spirits. Anything goes. You know what I mean?"

"No, I don't. What are you saying?"

She seemed to be searching for the right words, and then finally said, "Well, some of the guys here are, what you might call, unconventional. They don't really honor monogamous relationships."

"What are you trying to tell me? Be honest."

"If you really want to know... I've seen Dan acting very single and unattached for someone who claims to be so committed to you."

I could have asked her for examples, but I didn't want to hear any. My head was spinning. Clearly, Dan cared for me. Even Anne agreed to that. But, for whatever reasons, what he told me in the privacy of our time together was not what she'd witnessed when I wasn't around.

Once again I was losing footing on what I'd assumed was solid ground. I was devastated and began questioning everything. I knew I would have to confront Dan, but when I tried to talk to him, I couldn't stop crying and couldn't speak clearly about all that I was feeling, making it easy for him to evade my questions, deny my accusations, and continue to proclaim his love for me.

However, I no longer trusted him and was more confused than ever. Worse still, I hated the person I was becoming: the sort of woman I'd once vowed never to be. Helpless and needy. I recognized the pattern and despised it. I promised myself that this was not going to be my fate.

In the past, the secrecy surrounding Mother's illness forced me to question what was real and what was not. With Dan, I was once again questioning my reality. The thought of losing his love triggered memories of losses I hadn't ever fully acknowledged: the nurturing love of a mother who was present one day, gone the next; a brother whose departure for college left me alone with her; and a father who distanced himself from me because I was the girl, the one who would probably grow up to be a burden, like his wife.

Abandonment comes in many disguises, each bringing its own kind of pain, one no less devastating than the other. I couldn't help question whether I'd ever feel safe, even with those I loved.

When the humiliation became unbearable, I had to admit that Dan and I were headed for disaster. When we were together, it felt too much like when I lived at home, feeling as though I was on a roller coaster, dizzy and wanting to get off, but unable to do so.

I was frightened and needed to leave campus to clear my head. I called Herb and asked to spend the weekend with him and his wife. Their response was immediately comforting, and I quickly boarded a bus to Albany, transferred to another bus to New York, and took a cab to their apartment, where, before talking or eating, I collapsed onto their sofa. I knew about collapsing onto sofas. I had watched Mother do so time and again.

Although Herb was married and now had a child of his own, I still saw him as a substitute parent. I saw him as I needed to see him because I desperately needed help. Although I was concerned about how he'd view me—given my confused state, and knowing that he had dealt with our mother's emotional upheavals ever since he'd been a child—I couldn't let that stop me from asking for his advice. Fortunately, Herb's kindness, as well as Dee's, made it possible for me to unburden myself and not feel guilty about talking on and on about Dan. They listened, took what I said seriously, and suggested I speak to a psychiatrist. I didn't resist. I gathered what little courage I had and asked them to find a referral and schedule an appointment.

The doctor recommended to them had an office in one of New York's leading hospitals. The faded green corridor, coupled with the antiseptic odor of Lysol, reminded me of all the visits I'd made to see Mother in hospitals I could no longer name, in years I couldn't specifically identify.

As I entered the hospital, a guard pointed me toward a bank of elevators, saying I'd find the doctor's office on the seventh floor. A secretary, sitting behind a desk in a small waiting area, asked me my name and politely told me to take a seat. Then, just as I was beginning to consider leaving, the doctor appeared, nodded, and pointed me towards his office. He walked in front of me and spoke as he walked. Although we couldn't make eye contact, he lifted his voice in a questioning inflection, "Linda Appleman?"

My response was a mumbled but reluctant "yes." Inside his closet-sized office, he shut the door behind us, sat down, and pointed for me to sit opposite him in the only other chair in the room. I waited for a greeting but there was none. No hello. No smile. No introduction. All I could see was a balding head, dark-framed thick glasses over crossed eyes, and a white doctor's coat, which, half buttoned, revealed a big paunch resting on his desk. Knowing from Herb that I was in a troubled relationship, he got right to the point, firing a series of questions.

"So, Miss Appleman, tell me, are you and your boyfriend sexually compatible?"

How would I know? Dan was my first love. I hated the question, and I despised the questioner. Yet before I could find any words to answer, the next questions came: "Is he passive or aggressive with you, and are you passive or aggressive with him?"

I had never thought about such things, and I was even beginning to doubt the *doctor's* sanity. Then came the final assault: "Does your friend know how to please you as a woman?"

By then, I felt tremors throughout my body. I began to cry, twirled my hair, and fidgeted in my seat. All I could say was that I was feeling very sad, but I couldn't answer his questions.

"I don't understand what you're asking," I finally uttered, "and I don't know what any of that has to do with why I'm here."

His questions made my thoughts race, my heart thump. Images of Mother flashed before my eyes: an immigrant woman who must have suffered through many such inquisitions. The room itself further intensified the doctor's cold scrutiny. Windowless and tiny, the office had once-white walls that were now faded and bare, without color, with no sign of life anywhere. The stale air filling its space was as oppressive as the man himself.

I continued to sob, and at best I said a word or two more about my confusion. He remained silent. Then, with no emotion, he concluded, "Well, if you do think about the questions I've asked and decide you want to talk about them, call my office and make an appointment."

He didn't seem to care about the frightened, naïve twenty-one-year-old who couldn't tolerate his interrogation and who, despite feeling intimidated and humiliated, suffered through his drill. Once again, I didn't realize that I could have left at any time. I did, however, bolt at the exact moment he announced, "Your time is up."

Once outside the hospital, I felt like someone who has been wrongfully imprisoned and has just been released. Re-entering the world of the living gave me an indescribable sense of relief. I walked downtown instead of taking the bus, breathed in deeply, tasting the sun and the wind and noticing—as I'd never noticed before—how vast the sky appeared with its billows of majestic clouds. Armed with the decision that I would never again see that man nor go near his hospital, I felt saner than I had felt in weeks.

The euphoria I'd felt after leaving the doctor's office was short-lived. I returned to campus, managed to attend classes, and wrote all but one of my final papers. Yet, because my relationship with Dan continued to waver, visions of my mother resurfaced. Fears of becoming like her caused a frightening buzzing inside my head. I became depressed again, and pretending to be okay was no longer possible.

As life was becoming unmanageable, I was healthy enough—or desperate enough—to know that I needed professional help. Even though I didn't want to be seen walking into the college's counseling center, and I was unsure that I was ready to expose what had been happening, I needed to talk to someone.

The initial session set the tone for the half dozen times I met with a counselor before the end of the semester. The therapist, a woman in her fifties, greeted me warmly.

"It's good to meet you, Linda. Many girls cancel after calling for a first appointment."

"I almost did cancel," I admitted.

"I'm glad you didn't. It takes courage to come and talk with a perfect stranger."

I nodded in agreement.

"Please, have a seat," she said, pointing to a soft chair in her office. I was still nervous about what to say or where to begin, but she made it easy. Before I could ask, she said: "Talk about what you feel comfortable talking about. It doesn't matter where you begin."

"It doesn't?"

"No. Once you start talking, you'll find it won't be hard to continue, and it doesn't have to be painful or embarrassing. The idea is for you to feel better when you leave than when you came in."

She was eager to listen to what she later referred to as my "concerns," and her simple description of my anxiety began to reduce my stress. She made what I was feeling—what I considered a real depression—seem acceptable, worthy of talking about without someone thinking I was crazy.

As I began to talk about Dan, careful not to mention his name, tears came almost immediately. I confessed to feeling duped by the first guy I'd ever trusted and loved. Then my words tumbled out in a rush as I described having racing, obsessive thoughts that had been preoccupying me during classes, making it difficult to concentrate.

Her response was brief but reassuring. "Feeling duped in a relationship has to be one of the worst feelings for any young woman. I'm so sorry you're going through that, but it does explain why you're finding it difficult to concentrate. There's no mystery about that, Linda." It was important for me to hear that. Her understanding of my situation helped me disconnect it from my terror of following in Mother's footsteps.

We touched briefly on Mother and my childhood. There, too, her responses were sympathetic. She was affirming and respectful, and I left each session feeling that at least one person was beginning to understand me. Whatever questions she asked were posed in a way that freed me to answer them without feeling judged. After I told her that I'd be living and working in Manhattan during the upcoming nonresident term, she put me in touch with a psychologist, Dr. Goodman, in the city. He agreed to see me there, and with a stipend earmarked by the college for a student needing medical assistance, I met with him weekly, once again presenting my relationship with Dan as my major problem.

At the same time that I was working nine-to-five as a researcher and proofreader for a new international division of Encyclopedia Britannica, I was completing my senior thesis, a requirement for graduation from the literature division. My topic: "The Concepts of Love and Marriage in Tolstoy's Fiction." Ironically, at a time when my life was in upheaval, I poured hours of thought into the work of an author who, himself, had focused on the themes of love, war, and peace.

The introductory comments to my thesis included the following: "*My hope is to reflect upon some of the particular lives Tolstoy chose to create and write about, and in so doing to see the complexities, the demands, and the limitations, as well as the ideal imaginings of love and marriage, as he writes of them, as his characters live them.*"

I stated that in the first chapter my intention was to discuss young love as Tolstoy writes about it… "*where the unrefined feelings are still struggling for their identity, and reality is colored by a romantic imagination wherein the ideas of free love and necessity are, as yet, mutually exclusive and such a synthesis is therefore impossible."* A perfect example of understanding concepts intellectually and finding it impossible to apply them to one's own life.

Dr. Goodman's office was in an apartment building on Manhattan's East Side. His waiting room was decorated with soothing paintings and colorful, freshly cut flowers. I remember him being respectful, but I can't conjure an image of his face or the details of most of our sessions. I remember that he agreed to see me each week, charged a minimal fee, and said it was a pleasure to work with someone who was young, thoughtful, and wanted to be helped.

I began treatment with Dr. Goodman saying that I wanted to end my relationship with Dan, but didn't trust myself once I returned to campus. I knew how easily I'd be seduced by Dan's presence. It would be hard to resist the flowers he'd leave at my door, and despite believing it was in my best interest to do so, I doubted I'd be able to reject him.

Our last session was the most significant, and I remember it almost word-for-word. After saying goodbye, he looked directly at me and said, "Remember, Linda, you do have a choice. Even though your boyfriend will be at school, you don't have to date him. You don't have to spend time with him. If you do, that will be your choice."

I heard what he said, but as I feared, Dan's presence prevented me from separating and moving on without him. At that point in my life, I was simply not willing to accept the choice that would have meant living on the same campus, seeing one another at meal times, yet avoiding being with him.

However, the therapist's words were a gift that has stayed with me throughout the years. When I feel stuck, or when family members, friends, or patients feel that they can't move on, I return to what Dr. Goodman said: We each do have choices. Some are easier to make than others, but most of the time, we do have them.

As the soft breezes of spring replaced the chill of winter, Dan and I spent more time outdoors, making it all too easy to fall into old patterns and pretend nothing had happened to alter our love.

The sky, the sunsets, the dandelions, the lilacs all seemed to conspire against me, teasing me to see whether I took notice and would pick one flower, feel intoxicated by another, and in the end be swept off my feet by Dan again, incapable of logic, unable to focus on anything but the passion of the moment.

Even though I had said that I wanted to let go of Dan, there was a stronger impulse to enjoy the remainder of the term together, since we knew we would be parting after graduation. When the time finally came, we left each other in tears, with no promises, but without either of us able to say goodbye.

CHAPTER 22
DECEPTION, DENIAL, AND THE PATH TO HEALING

The summer after graduation, I traveled to the Middle East and Europe with Diana, my freshman roommate. It was 1963, my first time on an airplane and my first trip out of the United States. I paid for it with money I had saved from working summers in Manhattan, and from working at the college's switchboard, in the coffee shop, and as a babysitter during my four years on campus.

I had not applied to graduate schools and had no idea what I was going to do when I returned. With a liberal arts degree and a major in Russian literature, I didn't have many practical options. I knew only that I'd have to find a job, any job, but one that I hoped would at least be interesting.

What I did know was that I planned to enjoy the summer, my first real vacation, and the weeks abroad were—as I had imagined—splendid. The Italians thought I was Italian, the Spaniards were sure I was Spanish, the Greeks thought I was Greek, and the Israelis knew I was Jewish.

In most of the countries we visited—Israel and Spain, in particular—we were hosted by relatives, people introduced to us by college friends, or strangers we'd met along the way. We rarely stayed in hotels, and, when we did, we were lucky to find ones that were inexpensive and safe.

I wrote to Dan daily and received mail from him when we arrived in every major city. There'd be a bundle from him waiting for me, as well as a letter or two from my parents. Oddly, being so far away, conflicts that might have existed—knowing that my parents would never be accepting of Dan's not being Jewish—didn't affect my relationship with either of them. I remained blissfully happy, connected to everyone, though clearly and conveniently separating both allegiances.

One of the unexpected bonuses from the trip was my decision to apply to graduate school when I returned to New York. It happened only because I'd bumped into the same Bennington alumna three times in three different cities. Each time we'd have dinner together, she would talk endlessly about the graduate school she'd been attending, the Bank Street College of Education. "The school's philosophy is exactly what would appeal to you, Lin," she'd say. She'd talk about her student-teaching position in a private school in Manhattan, where teachers "loved to teach and children loved to learn."

So, while I'd never wanted to become an elementary school teacher—the typical job for Jewish girls in the 1960s—there I was, considering a very typical career, but at least in an atypical environment.

I applied for admission, sat for an exam, applied for a student loan, and was accepted within days after returning to the States in mid-August.

Classes began two weeks later. My first student-teaching position was at the Walden School on Manhattan's Upper West Side, where I apprenticed with a master teacher, Vida Hoffmann, who taught me more about how to nurture and respect children than I could have learned from any texts or any ten teachers combined. The true gift she gave me—and one I can't be sure she was aware of—was a way to nurture myself by being playful.

In modeling for me how to teach children in safe and respectful ways, she'd greet one student by saying, "I love the way you enter a room with that wonderful smile." To another, she'd add, "If someone said that to me, I'd be just as angry as you seem to be. Now let's see how we can best handle this situation." And when it came to playing, she was the best. "Oh, my, this sand box is just begging someone to dig his hands into it, to get all dirty, and to have so much fun that you'll either want it all to yourself or you'll want to tell all of your friends to join you!" She never scolded a child and always made someone feel good.

We taught third grade together, and our students were not, as in many of the city's private schools, simply children of the rich. Most of them had parents who were well-known actors, artists, and even a psychoanalyst or two. Having been a drama major for two years, and having survived Mother's illness as well as my own experience with an analyst, it was ironic that these were the children in my charge. Now I was offering counseling to their parents.

Vida taught me how to help the adults better understand the needs of their children. All of her lessons helped me as a mother helps her own children, but as mine was seldom able to do for me. She gave me insight into my own actions and reactions, and I learned something new about myself with each example she demonstrated, with every metaphor she told. Just as she was able to make even the most testy, obnoxious child feel good about himself, I, too, left school each day feeling that I had made a difference in someone's life, that I'd accomplished something worthwhile.

Midway through the year, I was asked to take over the sixth-grade class of a teacher requesting maternity leave. In what might have been a rash decision, I joined the faculty and never completed that first master's degree program.

Dan came to New York that spring to spend a week with me. Since graduating, we'd been writing and talking on the phone daily. The time was ripe for him to visit, to see where I lived, where I was making a life for myself. From concerts at the "Y" to art museums, dance recitals, Broadway musicals, and romantic restaurants, we couldn't do enough together or see enough of one another. Our time together was carefree and loving. On Easter, the day he returned to L.A., we waited together for his plane to board. He turned to me at the departure gate, pulled me toward him, and without any warning, he said: "I never thought I would be asking you this, but would you marry me, Lin? This past week was the very best week of my life, and I really do want to spend the rest of my life with you."

It wasn't your typical proposal. He didn't get down on his knees. There were no flowers or gimmicks, but it felt wonderfully honest.

Without hesitating, and feeling filled with new hope and so many dreams, I told him, "It's been the happiest week of my life, too."

We had no time to make any plans. There was just time enough for me to say "Yes," and for us to hug and cry, and hug some more.

A few weeks later, during my spring break, I flew to L.A. to sit for an exam that would qualify me to teach in California. I passed the exam, applied for a teaching position, and received one almost immediately. That time, too, was affirming of our love. I needed no further proof of his commitment.

Despite the fact that I had arranged to be married by a Reform rabbi and had convinced myself that I was prepared to live with the consequences of telling my parents after the wedding, I knew—some place deep inside myself—that they would never give us their blessings.

I told them nothing, and they were unaware that I had even made the trip to California before completing the school year at Walden. Then, after packing up my classroom, my colleagues all celebrated my departure, and I left them feeling successful and appreciated.

Before I moved to California, a handful of friends threw me an elegant dinner party. Herb and Dee, convinced that Dan and I had ironed out our problems, also offered their love and support, though they were still concerned about his not being Jewish.

My mother and father were spared from ever knowing about my final trip or my plans to marry. I was too much in love to consider all the consequences. So I left for California when they were away on a two-week summer holiday.

After leaving my life in New York and joining Dan to plan our wedding, I was once again caught off guard. In a matter of days, it became obvious that his main focus was on an upcoming concert in which he'd be dancing and choreographing. I didn't see that as a problem, as I was secure in his love for me. But everything came tumbling down when, in the darkness of a cool California night, some friends came to invite him to go out, and, thinking that I was already asleep, he left without a word.

Perhaps that would have meant little to someone who had not grown up as I had, but for me, in the moment I heard the door shut behind him, I knew that I'd never be able to survive not knowing what to expect, not fully trusting him to communicate openly and honestly. I knew, too, that his inconsistency and unpredictability were two ghosts I was unwilling to let back into my life.

After midnight, his mother and younger sister heard me crying and came downstairs to comfort me. They had been visiting him at the time, and I had grown close to them in our few weeks together. In fact, we felt ourselves to be kindred spirits, happy to be together, happy at the thought of soon becoming a family.

We talked for hours that night. His sister wrapped a knitted shawl around the two of us, and ultimately, those two women—his mother and sister—gave me the courage to leave. They alluded to knowing something about Dan that Anne had warned me about and that I had long ago put behind us—his inability to remain monogamous. Yet they cared enough about me, and were perhaps even ashamed of what had occurred, that they discouraged me from staying.

We cried and hugged, probably because we had already felt as though we were family. Yet when it was all too clear that it wasn't to be, I packed my half-unpacked bags and left quickly, while I still felt brave enough to do so.

I boarded a city bus at the corner and took it to the apartment of the only friends I had in Los Angeles at the time: my oldest childhood friend, Marion, and her husband, Sam. Although I was devastated, the healthy part of me knew I couldn't tolerate the compromises I would have to make if I married Dan. Had he come running after me, I don't know what would have happened. But since he didn't, I didn't think I had any other option. There was no time for closure or final goodbyes. I was too distraught, too fragile. I needed to return to all that was familiar, to family and friends who would offer love and support.

I had almost been willing to relinquish my role as Mother's caretaker only to be with someone who offered me an equally treacherous relationship. It was all too ironic and painful to contemplate.

I boarded a plane back to New York, sunglasses covering my red and swollen eyes. I desperately needed to understand how it could have happened: how I could have chosen the possibility of losing my relationship with my parents forever, while at the same time believing that a lasting change had actually occurred with Dan.

Once again, I turned to Herb and Dee. This time, Dee urged me to meet with a psychiatrist who was helping her deal with her own issues. I agreed to see him weekly, but unlike Dee, I didn't like his style. He doodled on a yellow pad while I cried through every session. There was no dialogue. I cried. He doodled. When he said, "Your time is up," I left.

He must have told me that I could call his service if I needed to reach him between sessions, because I do remember calling one lonely night when I felt flooded with anxiety and didn't know what to do. Shallow breathing led me into a cycle of fear, causing my head to spin, making it impossible for me to hold onto a single thought. Seconds into the conversation, he asked if I needed to be hospitalized.

"Of course not," I fired back. I was enraged. He thought I was crazy. I felt trapped and terrified. In a single moment, memories collapsed the past into the present and left me without a self that I recognized, trusted, or wanted.

I hung up and sobbed, feeling worse than before I had called. Admittedly, his questions made me realize I was ready to stop crying and begin talking, only not to him. He had become yet another man I could not trust, and I refused to be treated as a mental patient. It was painful enough to recognize that I was acting like my mother. I wasn't about to allow anyone to talk to me as though I was sick. I was scared and confused, true, but not sick.

Soon after returning to New York, my former employer, the principal of the Walden School, helped me get a job as a sixth-grade teacher in another private school. Since it was already late in the summer, I had just enough time to find a studio apartment and get my new classroom ready for the school year. I kept my sanity by staying busy and focusing on my tasks. When classes began, I buried myself in my work. Taking responsibility for the students and for what I taught them was in my control, and being in control was necessary for my mental health.

Unlike many of my colleagues who craved a social life after work, I seldom left when the final bell rang at the end of the school day. Instead, I worked with any pupil who needed extra help or met with parents who requested my advice about how to cope with their pre-adolescent sons and daughters. How weird was that? At twenty-three, unmarried, and with no children, I was confidently giving advice to parents who listened to me because of my title. I was the teacher and was, therefore, expected to have answers. Fortunately, I don't think I caused any lasting harm, but I learned a great deal about skepticism and humility.

When I returned to my apartment at the end of each day, I had lessons to prepare and papers to grade. I never left myself time to party, and that suited me perfectly, since meeting men was very low on my list of priorities.

In the city's single circles, I was definitely square. I didn't smoke pot, never tried any of the designer drugs, and at most drank a glass of wine or sipped a scotch on the rocks. I made a few poor choices, like leaving parties with guys I don't care to remember. The poorer my choice, the more convinced I became that no one was truly worthy of my time.

I still carried too much anger and ambivalence to feel at ease with any man, which made it impossible for me to project anything but hostility and sarcasm, even when perfectly pleasant men crossed my path. Wherever the authentic me was, she was quickly slipping out of my grasp.

No longer innocent or trusting, I didn't believe I'd ever love or be loved again. I also knew that if I continued to hold on to such beliefs, I would get myself into a deep emotional hole, from which it might be impossible to escape.

It would have been easy to blame Mother's illness for everything that was causing me pain, but I knew better by then. I knew that the hostility I felt toward men was poisoning the feelings I had about myself as a woman. I'd have to overcome it before I could begin to consider having a healthy relationship with anyone.

As with all wounds, healing took time. Finally, exhausted from wrestling with anxiety, tired of standing apart at social gatherings, and weary from simply being alone, I knew I was ready to talk to a professional therapist and once again try to make sense of my life.

This time I researched my choices thoroughly and took control of the kind of treatment I wanted. I went to the public library, read all that I could find about the different talk therapies available, then opened the yellow pages of the Manhattan phone book and ran my finger down the long list of mental health clinics throughout the city. After calling nearly every one of them, I found a few that offered to treat students at little or no cost, as long as the student agreed to work with an intern who would audiotape sessions and review them with a practicing clinician.

The application process was tedious and the waiting lists were long, but I was lucky. Within a week after submitting an application,

I received a call from the William Alanson White Institute on Manhattan's Upper West Side.

A therapist who was warm, respectful, and engaging encouraged me to begin telling my story. I told her about Mother, our family life in Brighton, receiving a scholarship to a prestigious college, and finally about my relationship with Dan. Her concluding remarks made me feel as though I'd found a part of myself I'd lost, perhaps on that Vermont path surrounded by the white birch trees.

She paused for what felt like a long time, then said, "Right now, you can't see beyond your vulnerability. Naturally, you feel frightened, because being vulnerable reminds you of your mother. But, you are not your mother. Throughout your childhood, your father's emotional health and influence must have been far greater than you realized for you to have survived as well as you have. Someday, you'll be able to embrace all of who you are. I hope we'll be able to assign someone to you very soon, so you can begin finding ways to get in touch with your strength."

I held on to her words, powerful words that are still with me today. For an entire year, I spent two lunch hours each week with a therapist who had the courage and wisdom to educate me about the mind and memory, and the capacity for change.

Meeting my husband-to-be, George, during that same year was no coincidence. It had been nearly two-and-a-half years since I'd left California. I was ready. Finally, I was beginning to see myself and the world through very different eyes. Therapy had helped me understand my relationship with Dan, and while I began to recognize that his unpredictability and lack of honesty showed he was not the person I should have married, meeting George proved that I could embrace a healthy relationship.

The night that George and I met was on the only blind date either of us had ever accepted, which wasn't, in fact, even a date. A mutual friend, Mary Kelley, who was working with George that summer, had four tickets to see *Man of La Mancha*, and she had offered two to George. At the last moment, the woman he was dating at the time couldn't come, so Mary called and offered me the ticket.

Another friend who had a car dropped me off early, and I waited underneath the theater's awning along with a handful of other people. Standing directly opposite me was a very handsome, tall, dark-haired young man with a distinguished mustache and goatee. As I found myself staring, I also convinced myself that some ugly, unimpressive woman would soon join him. Holding onto that thought, I lost him in the crowd that started gathering.

Then I heard Mary call out, "Lin, Lin, we're here." When I located Mary and her husband, I couldn't help but spot the man standing next to them. It was the guy I had been staring at. When I approached and she introduced us, we both laughed. Apparently, he had noticed me, as well.

Once inside the theater, we couldn't all sit next to one another. Three of us sat in one row, and George sat in the row in front of us. All I remember from the play is staring at George watching it. Afterward, we went into a small café for dessert. We talked about the city and our lives and, almost instantly, I realized that I hadn't felt so comfortable with a man in what seemed like ages.

As we were talking, Mary and I spotted the author Bernard Malamud walking by. "Bernie," as we both knew him, taught at Bennington when we were students, and each of us had known him. We called out to him, left our table, and chatted briefly in the street outside the café. It had seemed perfectly natural to me, but apparently it impressed George enormously. He was a big fan of Malamud's, and the fact that I knew him clearly made me seem more than merely interesting. When we returned, he launched into a discussion of one of Malamud's books and explained how reading it had affected his life.

At the end of the evening, the four of us shared a cab uptown. I expected George to wait, get out last with me, and escort me to my apartment. But, he did just the opposite. He got out first, offered a warm smile and simply said, "Bye, see ya."

I didn't tell Mary how disappointed I was, but every day thereafter she asked me whether he had called me yet. Apparently, as they were working together, he asked about me each day.

Then, early Sunday morning the following week, as I was reading the *New York Times*, Mary called yet again and asked, "Well, did he call?" At that point, I was thoroughly annoyed, and without thinking about it, I asked her for his phone number and dialed it seconds later. He knew exactly who I was after I'd said hello, and I boldly told him that I thought he was a coward. Why spend days asking about me and not contact me directly? He immediately said, "What are you doing today?"

I smugly responded that I expected to be seeing him. He then agreed to pick me up within the hour. As surreal as it may all sound, it felt perfectly natural.

We spent the next ten days seeing one another before he left for a theater company in Michigan, where he had been hired as a lead actor and director for the John Fernald Repertory Company at Rochester University.

I was happy to discover that George was well-read and intellectually curious, and shared many of the same experiences growing up as a first-generation Jew born to parents from Eastern Europe. And, yes, I was struck by how handsome he was. It was difficult parting not even two weeks after we had met and then having to endure a ten-month courtship long distance. Although we wrote and spoke frequently, he invited me to visit only once for a long weekend in December.

Until June, when he returned to New York, I was reaping the benefit of hours of ongoing therapy, learning to separate Mother's illness from my responsibility to myself and to set realistic expectations for my future.

As I learned what to expect in relationships outside the family, I explored the role I had played within my family. Eventually, I left sessions with a survivor's kit of tools: a sharper knife to cut out what wasn't important, a strainer to filter and savor what was, and a mirror to gain a sense of humor and true appreciation for myself and others.

George's plan was to return to New York in early June, after the theater's season ended. As May approached, though, I began to hear a hint of panic in his voice. Clearly, he had very specific notions about when he would be ready to settle down and get married, and he had not planned to make a commitment so soon.

Once again, I asserted myself. After work one day, armed with a glass of wine and no food in my stomach since the morning,

I told him that if he returned to Michigan for another year and expected me to sit around while he decided what to do, I had no intentions of waiting. Surely, I was taking a risk. But I had lived through enough to know what I wanted and decided that, at the very least, I would attempt to fight for him.

Luckily, my somewhat tipsy perseverance paid off. He proposed a few evenings later, ring in hand, in the lobby of the building in which I worked. And in his own state of shock, the first person he called to share the news with was his accountant. After laughing ourselves silly, we called our parents, and our engagement was official shortly after the Fourth of July weekend. We were married in late August 1967. Our families were ecstatic that each of us had chosen to marry someone Jewish, and our traditional wedding was filled with music, dance, and great joy.

George not only satisfied my need to be with someone in the arts, someone who loved theater, music, and literature as much as I did, but someone who, unlike Dan, didn't bring compromise or confusion along with his intellect and talent. With a regained sense of self-worth that came from being loved, I eventually found the courage to live life consciously, to make choices with my eyes wide open. That was and continues to be the gift that makes it possible to accept life's challenges and not become defeated by them. Acknowledging my strengths and making peace with my limitations have led me to a path where living consciously has made the difference between a life of mere survival, and one in which I take responsibility for what I can control, have the wisdom to admit what I can't, and the faith to be myself and to count my blessings.

CHAPTER 23
LIFE AFTER MARRIAGE

The first ten months of marriage were heavenly. We lived in a tiny cottage built on one of the old Dodge estates in Rochester, Michigan, where George continued to work as an actor and director in the same repertory company. I had expected to work, but when I was unable to find a meaningful job, I happily accepted the role of actor's wife, playing house, learning to hostess, and cooking gourmet meals.

After two months, Mother and Father came to visit for a long weekend in October, as George was about to open in the season's first production, *The Importance of Being Earnest*. In those days everyone dressed up for opening night, and Mother, Father, and I did so with delight. We sat in the third row of the orchestra, and since it was the first time they were about to see George on stage, they were curious and excited.

They were unprepared, though, to see their new son-in-law appear in a love scene in which he and the leading lady kissed. As their lips met, all those on stage—as well as those in seats around us—heard my soft-spoken mother exclaim, "Oooh, Moish, that's too long!" Father crouched in his seat from embarrassment, and I squeezed Mother's hand so tightly that the pain silenced her.

The company of actors joked about it for months, and Mother, too, was able to laugh about it after the performance. Yet even as she did so, it was clear she still felt protective of me. What happened on stage was very real to her. She politely concluded, "I know it's just a play, but still…"

Back in our cottage, it was easier to enjoy being a family. George worked hard to win Mother's respect, reassuring her of his love for me, while I played hostess to my parents for the first time in my life. It was so good to be able to entertain them rather than trying to take care of Mother.

Our days together ended much too quickly. I could hardly believe how happy they seemed to be with us, how relaxed they were in our little cottage, and how pleased I was to have them there with us. It all seemed so normal, almost too good to be true.

However, on the ride home from taking them to the airport, I was hit with a sense of foreboding I couldn't explain. Was it that nagging fear of a price to pay for good times? There was no way for me to share such thoughts with George. They weren't logical. I couldn't imagine him relating to such fears, not having grown up in my family.

Nevertheless, the price I anticipated came with a phone call. Only then it wasn't Mother's illness. It was Herb calling to say that Father had suffered another heart attack shortly after their return to New York. As in the past, he refused to be hospitalized. Once again, Dr. Andrews agreed to make daily house calls if Mother remained at his bedside. He felt Father would probably pull through. Even so, I was on a plane home the following day and stayed until I was convinced that Father was out of danger.

During my first phone call to George, he innocently told me that one of the actresses in the company invited him for dinner and that he'd just gotten back to our house. I was speechless. I wasn't at all surprised that any woman would attempt to spend time with him the moment I was gone. Since I'd been a teenager, I'd known that though female friends could be better than sisters, it was equally true that if one was out to win your boyfriend, she'd do anything to accomplish that goal.

George believed she was merely being thoughtful, but I was disappointed that he'd accepted the invitation. I thought he should have eaten alone the nights I was away. As a newly married man, it was not a time to be accepting a dinner date from a single woman. The fact that he did so left me with an all-too-familiar sense of betrayal. Just as frightening was seeing my internal alarm of abandonment sound so quickly. One seemingly innocent decision on his part, and my mind was off and running. So many snatches of memories were triggered, too numerous to recall each one.

I didn't worry Mother with my concerns about George. Instead, I told her how lucky Father was to have her. "No nurse would attend to his every need the way you do, Mother," I said. Her optimism about his recovery, I added, would surely help him regain his strength.

I left feeling assured that she was strong and in charge. Although he had taken care of her for much of her life, taking care of Father came easily and naturally for her when he needed her help.

Once I returned to Michigan, I called home daily until Father was back on his feet and back at work two months later. During that time, life with George was again filled with the excitement of the theater and adjusting to life as husband and wife. Most of our days were loving and tender, but with a lot of time to myself, no job, and no close friends, I often felt lonelier than I had anticipated.

I learned early in our marriage that I had no skills for dealing with conflict. Any disagreement became unmanageable, leaving me with no way to negotiate. Luckily, George found that unacceptable.

"No, you can't lock the door and stay in the bathroom sulking, just because we disagreed about something," he said during one of our first arguments. With patience and determination, he was the first man to prove to me that it was possible to disagree without risking the relationship.

We decided to return to New York at the end of the season. George pursued his acting career, and I landed an administrative position in the astronomy department at Columbia University. While life in Manhattan was filled with the stress of trying to make it in a big city, it was good to be back with family and friends. Some women I knew were pregnant or had recently had babies, and seeing them starting families awakened an urgency in me to do the same.

Despite financial worries, George agreed that it was time, and in a short while, I was pregnant, expecting a child in December 1969. I stopped working at the end of my fourth month, happily spending the remaining time planning for the baby's arrival.

What I didn't plan for during that time was the return of Mother's demons. With her medications, she'd been fairly stable since my sophomore year in college. I guess I believed the bad times were actually behind us.

On the surface, she appeared happy. She loved George, was convinced that we were having a daughter, and spoke of how she couldn't wait to cuddle the baby and be its grandma. But the Hitler devils returned. They crept out of the shadows in her mind, haunting her again. I heard the change in her voice when we spoke on the phone. Something was happening. What would George think if he witnessed it? How would it affect the two of us? Was it a coincidence that, like so many other times, she was losing control before a big event? Was her illness cyclical, chemical? Was it a switch that went off in her brain unrelated to anything, beyond her control? Whatever was brewing, it wasn't long before it would reveal itself. And when it did, my mother would again leave me at a critical time when I needed her.

In the middle of my eighth month, Mother agreed to meet me at Macy's to select a layette for the baby. The day started innocently enough. Mother had taken the subway into Manhattan and arrived on time, and she was able to conceal her agitation until we started to shop.

"I don't know, dear," she said. "Get whatever you think you'll need. Some receiving blankets, warm sleepers, a blanket for the carriage, some undershirts, nightgowns. Ask the lady at the counter, she'll help you."

Then she asked me to find a chair. "Maybe there's a place I can sit down. I'm feeling a little weak."

I found a cozy corner where she could sit and relax, and I ordered the layette myself. Not exactly the day I had hoped for, but I thought I should feel grateful that she was with me. We had a quick bite of lunch and, as planned for this mother-daughter day, we went to an afternoon showing of the film *Gigi* starring Leslie Caron.

As I sat next to her, I felt her body fidgeting, wriggling. I felt her elbow moving and knew that she was picking at her cuticles, something she only did when she was not herself.

When her anxiety became increasingly evident, I didn't know what to do, what to say, or how to address it. Instead, I did what I'd always done. I attempted to focus elsewhere, this time on the film, but my stomach began to ache and minutes passed before I realized I'd probably missed entire scenes. Then, catching me by surprise, Mother made a lively comment about the twinkle in Maurice Chevalier's eyes: "A real lady's man he is, even at his age, no?"

Hearing those few words, I tried to erase my fears. I even thought they were unfounded, that I was imagining something that wasn't true. But, seconds later, she was restless again, clearly anxious for the movie to end.

"It's very warm in here," she said. "Crowded. Very crowded."

By the time I walked her to the subway station, my head was throbbing. That familiar heaviness of spirit enveloped me.

I later learned that my father had called the doctor just the day before. He expressed concern about her sleepless nights, agitated mornings, and occasional incoherent mutterings. This doctor who had been medicating her for years reassured him. He had just seen her. She was taking her medication. He sensed no imminent danger.

The doctor was wrong. The next day Mother overdosed on pills after spiraling rapidly into that darkness that knew no bounds, where ending her life seemed the only solution. My father had sensed it. I had sensed it. But that wasn't enough to prevent what happened. She was rushed by ambulance to the hospital.

As in the past, we were as helpless as my mother was when confronted by the evil of her illness. We had no armor to offer her and none with which to protect ourselves.

I was immediately given medication so as not to go into premature labor and was also banned from any visits to the hospital. That left George, who had never before even seen Mother depressed, having to accompany my father and Herb to the hospital. For days, they stood constant vigil at her bedside.

She remained in a coma for nearly two weeks, during which time George refused to describe how she looked or the various monitors she was hooked up to that were keeping her alive. He protected me, sharing none of the shocking details of what he saw. At the same time, he somehow managed to help me focus on our unborn baby, attending Lamaze birthing classes with me and being as supportive as possible.

It wasn't until years later that he admitted to the disturbing images he carried around in his head: the tubes in Mother's throat to help her breathe, the whoosh of the respirator doing the breathing for her, the lifelessness of a person in a coma.

Yet, despite the horror that had to be dealt with, we made a conscious effort to hug each other, to notice a sunset, to focus on the future when there would soon be a baby in the borrowed crib that was inside our bedroom.

I knew the doctors had done a tracheotomy to enable Mother to breathe. After she came out of her coma, miraculously returning to the world of the living, she was transferred to Lenox Hill Hospital in Manhattan. Another tracheotomy was performed to correct what was termed "a botched-up job," and she remained in that hospital for two additional weeks.

Father's daily visits, as well as the entire experience, took its toll. He was rushed to the emergency room with chest pains. He had suffered a mild heart attack. He was given prescriptions to fill, but the doctors said he didn't need to be hospitalized.

We urged him not to stay home alone in Brooklyn, and he agreed to sleep in our apartment. For privacy, we gave him our bedroom, while we slept in the living room on a convertible sofa. I gave him his medications, cooked simple, non-fat meals, and at the same time attempted to care for myself and for the baby I was carrying.

George insisted that I schedule a session with the therapist I had worked with at William Alanson White. He wanted to ease the stress for me and avoid any possible complications with the pregnancy. I agreed and was able to meet with Dr. Fine two or three times before giving birth. He pointed out that, once again, I was proving that I could cope with catastrophe, but that I was taking my feelings "underground." Since I was succeeding in not thinking about Mother for long stretches of time during each day, he said that was good for the time being. He wasn't about to take away defenses that were protecting me.

He did suggest, though, that at some time it would be helpful to understand the family dynamics that flung me into such a role and forced me to survive in such a way. He marveled, he said, that I never once asked "why me?" or "why now?" I had clearly accepted the role of worrier and caretaker. Like the women in my family who had come before me—my grandmother, Ruchel, and, yes, my mother—I had learned to cope and accept and never question why.

My mother, her illness, the hospital, my father's heart attack— all had to be overcome. What other choice was there? After all, hadn't Mother been sick before? Hadn't the timing always been inconvenient? As long as she hadn't died, I forced myself to hold on to the idea of her living to be a grandmother. There was no time for self-pity or reflection. I simply had to get through each day, and I did so by attending to Father's needs and feeling grateful to George for being so helpful, and for not running away from this devastating package of my family that came with the woman he married.

I looked forward to the end of my pregnancy and the birth of our child. Keeping that image in the forefront of my mind, I continued to attend Lamaze classes and read every baby book I could get my hands on in order to do things right, to be the best mother I could possibly be.

Fortunately, in the 1960s my friends and I seldom thought about genetics and family predispositions to illness. At least, I never stopped to consider whether or not having children was a good idea given Mother's history. If I had, it probably wouldn't have mattered. I had already convinced myself that her depressive states were the result of early shock, loss, and abandonment. In the final analysis, I blamed medical ignorance for her recurring depressive episodes. I was also too preoccupied to worry about whether the stress I was experiencing could affect my baby, though I was assured that the medication I was given in those last weeks of pregnancy would not be harmful.

Now that Mother had once again sunk into the abyss, I was determined not to sink along with her. I wouldn't allow myself to become overwhelmed by feelings of despair. I had a baby to think about, and I was more determined than ever to end the complacency of the women who came before me, who not only had no say in their medical care, but who were victimized by a society that offered them little or no protection.

Two weeks before I gave birth, Mother was discharged from the hospital. As much as I wanted to see her and have both parents present for our baby's birth, I knew how weak she was, and I protected us both, perhaps for the first time.

I encouraged Father to take her to Lakewood, New Jersey, to convalesce. But I suffered their absence once the baby was born. Again, though, I wasn't aware of feeling anger, just terrible sadness.

After barely surviving a harrowing cab ride through the blizzard of Christmas Day 1969, I had an emergency C-section, and we were blessed with the arrival of our daughter, Keren. She was healthy, with a head full of dark brown hair and big brown eyes that seemed to say, "I'm here. What are you going to do for me?"

She sparkled with energy from the moment she entered the world and continues to do so to this day. I have no doubt she carries somewhere within her the stress and anxiety that had their roots in that terrifying last month of my pregnancy. How could she not have absorbed all that I was feeling, all that I was pretending not to feel?

When Mother and Father returned to New York, Keren was nearly a month old. The day they visited, I was a bundle of nerves. It seemed so long ago since I'd been to the movie theater when Mother and I saw *Gigi* together. On some level, it even felt as though she had died and was no longer a part of my life. I didn't know what to expect.

I was alone with the baby when the doorbell rang. As I held Keren in my arms, Father stood in the doorway with someone who bore little resemblance to my mother. She was at least thirty pounds thinner than I'd ever known her to be, and I wasn't prepared for the wig—a short one, with blond highlights—which sat askew atop her head, covering the bald spots where clumps of hair had fallen out during the weeks she'd been in a coma.

She wore a silk scarf around her neck, covering the open tracheotomy. Her soft voice was deep, gravelly, breathy. Gone forever were her soft and gentle tones. She had to put a finger over the open trachea, forcing the air through her vocal cords so that her words could be heard and understood.

As I sat next to her on the sofa, placing Keren into her frail arms, I felt the full impact of the tragedy that had again hit our family. I pitied the mother next to me and realized, more than ever, the price she was paying for another attempt at self-destruction.

Until that moment, I had done what I needed to do to give birth. Whatever I felt about my mother had been put on hold. However, seeing her face-to-face, I didn't know what to say or how to speak to her. She had missed the birth. She had missed Keren's first four weeks and, once again, I missed her being there for me. Yet we couldn't discuss any of it.

She had to continue to heal, find her way back into the world, before we could work our way back to being mother and daughter, before I could find ways to allow her to be the grandmother I so wanted my daughter to have.

I didn't know if that would be possible. Would I ever trust her to be alone with the baby? Would she have a relationship with Keren like she had with my nephew, Herb's son, Marc, whom she loved dearly? Would she ever again be able to relate to any of us? So many unanswerable questions swirled around in my head as I watched her looking at Keren, staring at me, looking so uncomfortable, out of place, uneasy within herself, uneasy with me, uneasy with my baby.

Linda, Abraham Lincoln H.S.
yearbook photo, 1959

Linda, graduation day,
1963, Bennington College

Linda & George on their wedding day,
August 27, 1967

Linda, Father, Mother, opening night,
The Importance of Being Earnest

CHAPTER 24
FATHER'S DEATH

Perhaps because Mother's health had always been our family's primary focus—hanging as it did on such a delicate thread—none of us ever seriously thought that Father might die before she did.

We worried about him, of course, but when he was sixty-nine and he and his partner decided to retire and close up shop, I suppose denial helped us avoid seeing what was in front of us: an increasingly paler, thinner, slower-moving man. At the same time, he seemed to have come to understand Mother differently. He had mellowed, and she welcomed the change.

In November 1970, Keren was nearing her second birthday. Father called one evening to say hello. It wasn't something he usually did. Mother was the one who stayed in touch and made the phone calls. However, he said that she was out and admitted to feeling lonely. So, we talked for more than an hour. Laughing, he recounted how he'd told each of his customers that week about his precocious granddaughter, Keren, who had affectionately called him a dirty old man. None of us ever figured out where she had heard that expression, but he had said something to her at Thanksgiving when we'd last been together, and with a great big smile on her face, she said, "Grandpa, you're a dirty old man!" It tickled him, and never for one moment did he find it insulting.

He talked, too, about retiring and having ambivalent feelings about not working. As he began to talk about looking forward to traveling, he interrupted himself, and, much to my surprise, he said, "Who would have thought you would have turned out to be the strong one, Linda? The one I could depend on? Herb's always busy with one project or another, but you, I know I can count on you to take care of Mama. That I don't have to worry about."

I heard that as an affirmation, a recognition of my strength and my character that he respected. Knowing that he believed I could care for Mother felt more like a vote of confidence than a burden. It was a gift. He had expressed his faith in me, much the same way as he had expressed his faith in my ability to make dinner for him years earlier.

I slept peacefully for a while that night. I had gone to bed relaxed and contented, but I awoke with tears streaming down my cheeks around three in the morning, after a nightmare in which Father had died. Confused and alarmed, I shook as George held me. Eventually, I fell back to sleep.

In the morning, I met a friend and together we went to Riverside Park with our children in strollers. As I sat on a bench near the sandbox, chatting and watching them, I saw Herb running toward us. He and Dee lived in the same apartment building as we did on Manhattan's Upper West Side, and it was clear from his expression that something terrible had happened.

Before I could say anything, he asked my friend if Keren could spend the day with her. "Lin and I have to go to Brooklyn. Our Dad's been taken very ill."

The rest happened so quickly that there wasn't time to grasp it all. Within half an hour, the two of us were on the subway heading for Brooklyn. Not until then did Herb say, "I got the phone call only minutes before I came down to the park to find you. Mom gave the hospital my number. They called her first, but she doesn't know yet."

My mind began to race with thoughts of this being Father's last week at work, the week that he was selling all the unsold papers, twine, and office furniture, as well as closing the books. He and Mother planned to travel to Israel, to visit relatives in Florida, to see more plays and films.

Then I heard myself ask, "But she doesn't know what yet?"

Herb started to sob. Sitting in the BMT subway car, my brother was sobbing. The call, he said, had come from someone in the hospital's morgue. They needed someone to come identify the body.

"Dad's dead, Lin. He had a heart attack. They said he died like he said he always wanted to die, with his boots on. He was at work, got off the phone, slumped over, and fell down. And that was it."

In a way, I had been eerily prepared. I had done my crying in the middle of the night when I dreamed of his death. Yet once we arrived, it was Herb who identified Dad's already cold body in the bowels of the hospital, the sub-basement where the morgue was located.

I was sent to an office where I filled out next-of-kin papers stating where the family wanted the body to be moved. Taking care of the facts was something I could do, something much easier than confronting death head-on. Filling out the forms helped to ground me. My father was no longer alive. That was the first fact. Second, the body, as the form referred to him, had to be transferred to be prepared for a religious burial.

When Herb returned, his eyes still red, his figure more stooped than straight, I could no longer hold myself together. "It wasn't supposed to happen this way," I said, between sobs. "For the first time he and Mother were going to spend time together, not worry about business, about bills, about us."

"He wasn't supposed to die before Mom, Lin. He could have taken care of himself, lived on his own."

In the subway, on our way to break the news to our mother, we each sat, rocking gently, our minds traveling through time, choosing memories or picturing the future without Father. I imagined the scenes Herb must have been revisiting: the years of being Father's big boy, the son Father always leaned on, saddling him with the responsibility of admitting Mother into hospitals and staying with her during her shock treatments, saying that he couldn't do so, claiming the doctors wouldn't listen to him because he wasn't American. His English wasn't good enough. So, when Herb was very young—probably ten or so—he had been pressed into service as Mother's caretaker. Of course, I knew none of this until I was well into adulthood. Yet it still struck me as ironic that Herb seemed angrier with Mother than with Father. I never understood why it wasn't the other way around.

As we neared the stop for Sheepshead Bay, the tension mounted. Each of us was wondering how to tell Mother and how she would react. Would she fall apart instantly? Would it trigger a long-term depressive episode? When she saw us there together, in the middle of the week, in the middle of the day, our faces transparent masks of sorrow, she knew something awful had happened. It wasn't necessary to speak, yet of course, we had to say something.

"What's the matter? What happened?" she repeated, before Herb could tell her. Once the words were out of his mouth, she turned ashen.

"*Oy, Got,*" she repeated in Yiddish, the language she reverted to whenever she was upset. *Oh, God.*

We took turns hugging each other and crying. When she started to tremble, we got her a cup of hot water to drink and a sweater for her to put over her housedress.

"I'll be of no use to you. I'm too nervous. Please do whatever has to be done. Get a plain wooden box. That's what the Orthodox do. That's what Daddy would want. Nothing *oongapatchkit*, nothing gaudy."

After a long pause, she continued, "But he kissed me on the cheek just this morning before he left. He said, 'I'll see you later, Miriam.' Some later! How can it be? Did you see the body? Do you know for sure?"

Without waiting for an answer, she walked into her bedroom, picked up her wedding picture, stared at it, and said aloud, "No more Moish! Now you're gone, too. Gone. One, two, three, boom. Just like that."

Herb made the official phone calls and arrangements, and I called the relatives. We stayed at Mother's house that night, but none of us slept. We each lay in our beds—the same beds we slept in as children—unable to comfort each other or ourselves.

CHAPTER 25
MAJOR CHANGES

I had shared my mother's history with George soon after we'd met, admitting that I would feel responsible to take care of her if my father died before she did, though I didn't think that would happen. Remarkably, he accepted my explanation and didn't seem to think of it as a burden.

We never spoke about it again until after Father died. Then, too, he agreed that it would be in Mother's best interest to live with us. We couldn't abandon her. Herb and Dee each worked full-time, and Mother was far too young, at sixty-four, to be placed in an old-age home.

Our preference was to find a large apartment in Manhattan, but Mother soon made it clear that such a move would be difficult for her. She needed to be in her neighborhood, where everything was familiar and where she wouldn't have to make too many changes.

Of course, she would have preferred to live on her own and to remain in her apartment, but she recognized what we all knew. Given her history, that wouldn't be wise. And since I had promised Father I would take care of her, I felt obligated to honor that promise. Also, in the weeks after his death, I'd spent so much time taking the subway to Brooklyn to keep her company or had her spend weekends with us in Manhattan, that living together seemed the most practical solution.

To make the decision easier for her, we told her how much she could help us by living with us. She could contribute toward the rent and other expenses and also help care for Keren. In the end, we convinced ourselves that it would work, that it was the best alternative.

We rented the top two floors in a spacious house in Manhattan Beach, where there seemed to be more than enough space. We gave Mother the master bedroom with its own porch. Once we readied ourselves for the move, I had to pack our apartment and help Mother organize and pack hers. I had little time to mourn Father's death. I thought of him, of course, and one way I felt I could honor his memory was to have another child and give him a namesake. It would also give me someone else to take care of and less time to think about the complexity of our lives.

Was I following a pattern? I remembered the story Mother told me of Dr. Andrews telling her to become pregnant as a way to lift her spirits. Was it more than a coincidence that I was then wanting to have another child? Probably.

Luckily, becoming pregnant wasn't a problem, and compared to my pregnancy with Keren—when I had to contend with Mother's suicide attempt, her absence from me, and her stay in an intensive care unit—my second pregnancy was merely exhausting.

It was soon after our move from Manhattan, and I was also unaware of all that I was concealing from myself.

George was supportive and loving, but he was rarely at home. That left me alone with Mother and Keren, and I didn't realize how much I was affected by Mother's daily routine—staying in bed late and coming down in her nightgown or an old housedress to watch soap operas at noon. Finally, a friend visited, saw Mother, and confessed that if she had to live with a mother who was so depressed, it would drive her crazy.

Clearly, I had simply been ignoring my own depression. Now, after it was pointed out to me, I was determined to devise new house rules. Mother would have to get fully dressed if she wished to come downstairs for the day. She was also to comb her hair and put on makeup.

We bought a television for her bedroom, so she could watch her programs in privacy upstairs and dress when she wished. These changes turned out to help all of us.

I also needed to address the separate lives that George and I were beginning to lead. Seeing other husbands and wives shop together on the weekends awakened feelings of resentment and sadness, since we seldom had the time to enjoy even simple, mundane pleasures together. In fact, we had very little time for ourselves at all.

It didn't matter that everyone seemed to envy me for being married to an actor. The actor I was married to was in matinees Saturdays and Sundays, and performing Saturday nights. Often, just to see him, I drove into Manhattan and picked him up after an evening's performance. I'd tell myself I wasn't too tired and that it was worth it, when in truth I was exhausted, having spent the day caring for the house, cooking, serving dinner, bathing Keren, and getting her to sleep before leaving for the city around ten.

George's only day off was Monday, a school day, which didn't really give us the day for ourselves. In the evening, none of our friends wanted to go out. "But it's Monday," each one said. They went out on weekends. So our social life—or at least mine—was anything but normal.

Keren, at two, clearly felt much of the stress of her Grandpa's death, and had to adjust to a new house and neighborhood in Brooklyn, as well as to Mother's moving in with us. After that, she was faced with my pregnancy and the birth of a sister. We saw our inquisitive, bright little girl showing signs of anxiety. She lost her temper quickly and also seemed to lose her playful innocence and humor. She became withdrawn in public and explosive at home. We did our best, but we were ill-equipped to meet her needs.

Once our second daughter, Mia, was born, we had another beautiful addition to our family, someone else to care for, who allowed me to bury any discontented feelings. Mia had one advantage that Keren hadn't had. She was born into the family when Grandma was a part of it, and though she had an older sister who was tempestuous and precocious, she chose, at a very early age, to be the caretaker of us all.

Whenever tensions in the family erupted, she waddled away and hummed or sang aloud in another room, tuning us out and creating her own private place of comfort. Then, to make us all feel better, she'd return, smile, giggle, hug us, and amuse us. Her presence was always healing. None of us could respond to her with anything but joy. Yet in doing so, we unwittingly silenced her, encouraging her to continue in the role of rescuer. It was a heavy price, not one that any of us was aware of until she was too old for us to go back and undo what had been done.

With the benefit of hindsight, we could see, as most parents do, what we would have done differently with each of our daughters. We would have helped Keren to feel less deprived of our attention and less in need of receiving it in negative ways. We would have encouraged Mia to be less perfect and less focused on caring for others.

The decision to have Mother live with us was, in many ways, stressful for the girls and for our marriage. Too often, I gave Mother more attention than I gave the girls or George. I didn't know how to live any other way. I was plugged into Mother's every mood, and I responded to her as I always had.

With my daughters, I tried to make up for much of what I had never been given. I hosted extravagant birthday parties. I was active in the school PTA and offered each of them ballet and piano lessons with the best teachers I could find. In later years, I drove Mia, who expressed a passion for dance, theater, and music, to classes and summer theater camps.

I believe that certain templates for our personality—our likes and dislikes, as well as our vulnerabilities—are set into motion early in life. But it's also true that if gone untreated, stress and other negative influences can hinder growth.

I may never know whether my love has eased any of the hardships our family has endured. I can only hope that my husband and daughters trust the insights I offer about their own choices and challenges.

CHAPTER 26
REDEFINING MYSELF

While living in Brooklyn with Mother after Father's death, I volunteered for organizations, served on a variety of boards, and edited an alumni magazine for Bennington College. The days were full and busy, but what I felt lacking was a professional identity.

After we had our two daughters, George joined the faculty of a prominent acting school. After a few years, though, the desire to return to performing led him to join a summer theater, the Williamstown Theatre Festival in the Berkshires, where he shared the stage with Ken Howard, Olympia Dukakis, Blythe Danner, and Geraldine Fitzgerald.

Keren was six-and-a-half, Mia three. We planned to have a wonderful summer. I enrolled Keren in a day camp and Mia in a morning preschool program. Yet, once again, I had no niche of my own, and the summer turned out to be unexpectedly painful. I longed for more than playing the role of actor's wife and mother.

As I waited for George to leave rehearsal at the end of a hot summer day, I stood with both girls, sweltering alongside another parent, a tender, friendly man. It turned out to be Bruce Paltrow, waiting for his wife, Blythe Danner. He stood with his two children, a son, Jake, and a daughter, Gwyneth. We chatted about being "the summer spouse" and about living in New England.

Moments later, the cast emerged. When she saw me with her husband and discovered who I was, Blythe spoke to me.

"So," she said. "What do you do?"

That was the killer line. The question immobilized me. I couldn't even say with pride that I was the mother of my two beautiful girls, that I was active in many organizations, or even that I was enjoying a vacation away from home. Clearly, her question was innocent enough, but filtering it through my own insecurity, it silenced me.

Her question, though, spurred me to realize that I was not happy with the limits I had accepted for my life. I had been feeling increasingly frustrated, but as had been my habit, I took all such feelings underground. The stress might have contributed to the breakdown in my immune system the following winter, when I was hospitalized. A horrible flu had left all my joints terribly swollen. After I'd been poked and prodded and X-rayed for days, I was finally diagnosed with the autoimmune disease sarcoidosis.

Being hospitalized for more than two weeks and separated from the girls was difficult enough. The real battle was the need to be hyper-vigilant, even while in the hospital. The staff made frequent mistakes, forcing me to keep records of every pill administered, ensuring they were the right medications at the correct dosages. It was disturbing to see that even while in a hospital, I needed to stay in control of the situation, focusing on the responsibilities of others when I was the one in need of care.

It took my body four months to fully recover, during which I re-evaluated who I was and who I wanted to be. The experience served as a wake-up call for me to do something meaningful with my life.

At first, I took a part-time job managing a special group of immigrant musicians recently allowed to leave Russia. I helped them form an orchestra and scheduled performances throughout New York and New England. I wrote grant proposals, received funding from the National Council on the Arts and other city and federal agencies, and often accompanied the group, acting as producer and director.

My hours away from home, functioning in an adult world where I was once more helping people, revitalized my spirits. When the grant money dried up, though, it was time to move on.

This time, it was Mother who came up with the solution.

"You've always been happiest when you've been in school. Why don't you take some courses, dear. I'll help with the girls as much as I can. Trust me, mamaleh."

It made perfect sense, and Mother *was* there. Within hours, I called Bank Street College, where I'd studied for my master's degree in education, and asked them to send me their summer catalog. Two classes called out to me. One was titled "The Gifted Child," and the other was a course in "Adolescence." Both girls were clearly gifted, and Keren, at ten, was already acting and thinking like an adolescent. This would help me understand them, while I got credit toward another degree, if I wanted to continue.

Soon after classes began, I was encouraged to become one of the first students to pursue a degree in the college's new counseling and human development department. I met my mentor for life, Ruth Hersh, a woman of endless resources, who always pointed me toward new areas of learning. It wasn't her brilliant lectures that singled her out from all the other faculty members. It was all the programs, workshops, concerts, and art shows that she insisted we attend. Among them was a Balinese dance group, a book signing for an up-and-coming author, a new two-year course in neuro-linguistic programming.

Ultimately, my major led to a graduate thesis in oral history, which included two oral histories, one of my mother and another of my mother-in-law, with color-coded genograms—similar to family trees—at the end of each one. As an oral historian, I have since documented the lives of several elderly people in New York, as legacies for their families.

In the end, Mother proved to be right. I thrived in school, and I added to my degree in human development by receiving certifications in neuro-linguistic programming, Ericksonian hypnosis, and addictions counseling.

In retrospect, each of the personal and professional choices I've made—starting with being a camp counselor in my teens to teaching in my twenties—was directly related to those early, formative years in our home, where the need for balance was essential, where mother's emotional turmoil made caregiving a way of life. I was a child in terms of age, but I didn't move through the world as children in more normal households do.

In high school and college, friends often sought me out, sharing their private thoughts and asking for advice. I assumed I was merely being a good friend when I took the time to listen and process their concerns, doing what needed to be done, what the situation called for.

As a therapist, I treat my patients with the same respect I would show any guest in my home. I ask no one to leave a session if we're in the middle of a critical conversation, because I believe that my priority must be the health of the patient. I have had patients for whom remaining in denial was lifesaving. For others, examining memories—especially with the help of a professional—has been life-altering, easing the pain of the original assault and allowing the patient to discover healthier coping skills.

I see myself foremost as an educator. The course being taught is the self, and when patients succeed in passing, the skills they gain transform their lives. I share parts of my life story only if I feel it will be helpful.

Though I'd been conceived to make Mother happy, I don't see my work as a therapist as a form of needing to make others happy, so much as it is to help them change harmful behaviors. But I still do need to help.

When I'm able to help an adolescent feel empowered while living in the midst of chaos, or when I teach a couple how to rekindle the love and respect they once had for one another, or I am able to lighten the burden of a single parent or the spouse of a recovering addict, helping each to get in touch with strengths and options, I know that I am making a difference.

As difficult as my childhood was, I see it now as a gift from which I can draw strength and compassion. I evolved into the person I am today as a result of that gift, and much to my relief and gratitude, I am no longer invisible.

Newborn Keren

Keren's last time with
Grandpa, 1970

Linda, after Father's
death, 1971

Linda & young Keren

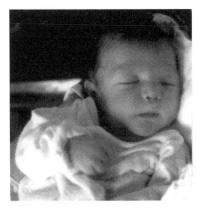

Newborn Mia

Baby Mia with Linda

Mama Linda & her girls

Keren, age 7

Mia, age 5

CHAPTER 27
THE LAST TIME

In 1982, we decided to move. Keren was about to enter high school and Mia middle school. We were tired of renting and wanted to own our own home. We focused our search in Westchester County, a suburb north of Manhattan.

For Mother's benefit, we looked at houses that were near public transportation and finally bought one that was a minute's walk to a bus stop, so she wouldn't have to rely on us to drive her every time she wanted to get out.

For us, the move was good. We welcomed the change in scenery and were beginning to enjoy the physical space of the suburbs, as well as the foliage—the trees and lush colors that surrounded us—but the change wasn't good for Mother. From day one, she became easily disoriented, then frustrated, then agitated. "I can't find my way around," she'd say, unable to remember how to get from one part of the house to another.

The girls, too, were beginning to welcome their newfound independence, carving out new lives for themselves, so they no longer needed Grandma as a babysitter. That, too, added to Mother's feeling displaced.

Within days of the move, she seemed ready to slip into a full-blown depression. I drove her into Manhattan to meet with a psychiatrist friend, and by session's end, we all agreed we'd have to find another living arrangement for her. I visited several facilities and finally decided to call one known as The Country House. It was less than half an hour north of our new home. We took her for a tour of the grounds and its facilities and, weeks later, she decided to move in.

During the year she lived there, she had a peer group of her own for the first time since before her marriage. She had friends who admired her, and she told us that she felt dignified and respected. Being with people her own age and having no real responsibilities afforded her the pleasure of feeling like a lady again. Being served three meals a day in a bright, handsomely decorated dining room and needing to care only for herself seemed to suit her. I talked with her daily and visited weekly. On Thursdays, when a van brought the residents into town, I'd meet her for lunch at Macy's.

The following year, though, during one of our morning phone conversations, I heard something strange in her voice. When I asked if anything was wrong, she hesitated, then quickly asked, "Can I spend just a few days with you? Can you pick me up, mamaleh?"

"When?"

"Today. Can you come now?" That was her simple, immediate request, and I couldn't refuse.

I drove north to get her, but I hardly remember how I got there. Fear colored every image, every thought. Her last suicide attempt, during my first pregnancy, loomed large. I was still adjusting to our new home, attempting to make new friends, develop a new practice as a psychotherapist, and cope with Keren's not-so-easy adolescent years. As when I was pregnant with Keren, Mother's struggles hit me at a critical time.

If there was a trigger for this crisis, I thought I knew what it was. I'd taken her to an ophthalmologist in Manhattan the week before, and after a series of grueling tests, the doctor diagnosed her with macular degeneration. To that, he foolishly added that she might eventually lose her vision. Her panic was immediate. She fidgeted during the entire ride home, more anxious than I'd seen her in years.

"My eyes give me what few pleasures I have, Linda. Watching my television shows, reading the paper, a good book, taking my daily walks, being able to see trees and flowers and the sunshine. What else do I do?" After a pause, she asked simply, "What will happen to me now?"

Surely, she must have questioned whether life would be worth living without her sight. No doubt, she was reminded of her blind Tanteh who died after years of living in The Hebrew Home for the Aged.

The moment she entered our house, she crawled into bed and stayed there. "Just let me rest, mamaleh," she begged. But the next morning, I was tough. She had to get up, eat breakfast, get dressed, start the day. She had to go outside, take a walk with me. Move, breathe in the crisp air of late September, watch the orange-red leaves of fall dance to their special rhythms.

Arm in arm, we began to walk. I aimed for a mile and hoped she wouldn't tire after a few steps. Then, I saw that helpless, vacant stare, the one I hadn't seen in years.

She wasn't seeing the trees or their leaves. We weren't breathing the same air. I knew it, and still I prayed that what I was sensing wasn't real. When she interrupted the small talk I was attempting to engage her in, my body became rigid. "I never thought the black clouds would return," she said. "I never thought they would." A shiver passed through me. I knew then that I, too, had believed those clouds would never return.

For the first time in my life, I felt it would be kinder, for her and for all of us, if she didn't have to suffer one more time. Why fight again? I knew she had already begun to slip into her darkness. The doctor's words had, no doubt, haunted her with images of life at its worst: needing total care, living in a nursing home or back with us, each option unacceptable.

So she did what her body knew how to do. She allowed depression to envelop her. The diagnosis had triggered fear, and the fear brought out her demons once again. Only this time I couldn't allow her back into our lives. I knew that I wouldn't survive.

I called Herb in Michigan, where he had accepted a position as a college professor at the same university where George was a member of the repertory company. Dee taught in a private school, and their son, Marc, was already away at college.

"I can't believe it," I told him. "She's been doing well for so long, but it's not good, Herb. She refuses to get out of bed."

I pleaded with him. "I don't have the energy to nurse her back to health this time. Please, let her stay with you for a while."

"Do you think she'll need to be hospitalized?" he asked.

"I don't know."

He paused. I waited. "Okay, kid," he finally said. "Make the arrangements. Let me know what flight she'll be on. Maybe the change will do her good."

When I drove her to the airport, we barely spoke. Clearly, she hated me for handing her over to Herb as much as I hated her illness that was separating us once again.

The next time I saw my mother, she was in shrouds, her body ice-cold in the plain wooden casket in which she was buried. She had been hospitalized for depression, but she had been released. The discharge summary from the hospital reduced Mother's life to: "Patient, a seventy-three-year-old, white female with multiple hospitalizations, a long history of depressive episodes since age twenty-five, numerous psychiatric hospitalizations treated with electric convulsive therapy and antidepressant therapy. There is no history of mania. There is a history of a postpartum psychosis."

The irony is that she did not die from the ravages of mental illness. She had not attempted suicide. She was back with Herb and Dee in their home and was due to return to New York Thursday.

We spoke the Sunday before. Mia was home and had been able to speak with her. She told Mother how much she missed her and loved her. Before saying goodbye to me, Mother asked that I schedule a beauty parlor appointment for the following Friday.

The next day, Monday, in the middle of the night, I was awakened from a dream in which a physician in a white coat invited me to witness a person dying. In the dream I told him that I was a coward and had no desire to watch anyone die. He insisted. "When someone is ready to die, death is very peaceful. It's an extraordinary experience. The patient here is calm. Death will be natural and easy. Watch and you'll see."

After I listened to his words, I found myself in a small room. The patient was lying on a narrow bed, a cot. I then witnessed something remarkable. A beatific expression came over the person's face. Death was quick, easy, peaceful. The dream ended.

I awakened George, shaking, and told him that I didn't know why I had such a dream. "You're probably thinking about your father at this time of year," he said. I considered that a possibility.

However, in the morning, after we were both fully awake, I began to have horrible stomach pains. I was so uncomfortable that I went to see our family physician, who concluded that I was experiencing what seemed like an ulcer. Since it was my first episode, he advised waiting before taking any tests. He suggested an over-the-counter remedy and told me to stay in touch.

Later that afternoon, Herb called from Michigan. Without saying hello, he said, "Sit down, kiddo." Then he began to cry.

"I had breakfast with her this morning. Then I left to teach a class, and when I came home at lunchtime, she was already dead. She was on the bed in my office, the room we set up for her. The doctors said she died from a perforated ulcer."

"Hadn't she complained about her stomach hurting while she was in the hospital?" I asked, not yet taking in what he'd just said.

"Yes, and she was told to check it out once she returned to New York. But what's the use of talking about that now? She's gone, Lin. I'm in the midst of making preparations for the body to be flown back to New York. You'll have to make all the burial arrangements, go to the funeral parlor, select the casket, call the family. I'm trying to book a flight for Dee and Marc and me for tomorrow morning."

"Okay. Don't worry," I said. "I'll take care of everything." I didn't bother telling him about my dream—the small room, the small bed—or my aching "ulcer."

When I told my daughters, Keren's first response was, "You're an orphan now, Mom."

"Don't be silly. I'm a grown-up," I said. Of course, she was right. Within moments, I felt bereft, totally alone. My mother had been an orphan at fourteen. At forty-four, I was now one, as well.

If it hadn't felt as though she'd died so many times before, her actual death would have been harder to accept. It would have been harder yet, had I not had my dream the previous night.

Since neither shock nor loss were new companions, I handled Mother's death as I'd learned to handle life—not because I was brave or especially wise—but because, like most people at such times, I did what I needed to do to survive.

Now, more than two decades later, I still mourn for the mother I never had and the mother who was mine and mine alone: a beautiful, fragile, loving woman whose face I now see when I look in my morning mirror or when I catch a glimpse of my reflection in the glass of a storefront.

Even when I'm not thinking about her, she's with me. A shadow beside me. She's a part of who I am—the best of me and the rest of me.

George & Linda

Keren & Mia
(photo by Laurie Lichtenstein)

AFTERWORD

I did not start out to write a memoir. I had three careers before I studied and trained to become a psychotherapist, and at the time this seed was planted, in the mid-1990s, I had been in private practice for more than twenty years and had been working at an outpatient facility for addicts and their families for nearly ten.

It was at a time when I found myself suggesting to my patients that they read one of the many self-help books that were then beginning to fill the marketplace for adult children of alcoholics and nearly every other addiction. I realized that few had been written for adult children of the mentally ill, and I decided I could help fill that void.

I didn't get past the first few pages, though, when I realized I would leave the self-help books for others to write. I had a story to tell about growing up with a mother who suffered from bouts of major depressive episodes, and felt that sharing it would be a more important contribution.

I knew from the start that I did not want to write in my psychotherapist's voice, but thought it would be more valuable to readers to recreate the world I lived in, allow the people in my family to speak for themselves, and show the effects of living with a parent who was ill.

To help myself in the process, I decided to visit the neighborhood in which I spent my early years and visit the house in which so much of the chaos I experienced took place.

New York's newspapers were featuring Brighton as "The New Odessa," a neighborhood where houses were being restored and revitalized by a wave of new immigrants—mostly Russian, some Korean. I needed to return, hoping that my house would be one that had been restored, and that I would be able to see it. I went with a camera in hand and my older daughter, Keren, twenty-five, at my side.

I parked on Brighton Beach Avenue and walked to the corner of 2nd Street. Much to my delight, our house was there. The steps leading up to the front door were cracked, the stucco had been recently painted.

I summoned the courage to ring the front doorbell, and we were greeted by a young Korean man. I told him I used to live there and asked if we could come in. He smiled graciously and asked us to wait for a few moments before he could let us in.

Keren and I walked toward the alleyway, which she had seen in the only photo I have of myself at age two, wearing a white summer pinafore and standing in front of the door leading to the basement apartments. She insisted that I pose in front of that same door. "You look so cute, Mom," she said as took a photo. The man returned and invited us inside.

As I walked through the four rooms of my childhood home, memories returned. At first I saw our family sitting peacefully at the dinner table, but that image gave way to another: I had been awakened by Father shouting at Mother. I heard her racing frantically in and out of every room, her speech garbled, her body a shadow on my wall cast by the bathroom light.

My daughter sensed my preoccupation. "Mom, you okay?"

"I'm fine," I said, slowly returning to the present.

"You sure?"

She slipped her hand into mine as I took a deep breath, forced a smile, and told her, "It's okay. We can go now."

As we walked away, the burden of memories lingered. I knew that I would have to revisit parts of my past that I had successfully buried. I had no illusions about being able to make peace with what might emerge, but I also knew that I needed to make my pictures whole.

With what we now know about family dynamics and how children are affected by a parent or sibling who is ill, it's easy for me to see why it's always been difficult for me to be spontaneous or carefree. I had learned early to behave as an adult, with an exaggerated sense of responsibility, vigilant at all times.

As one witness to the human capacity for pain and survival, I hope my story speaks to the many adult children who grew up as I did, during the years before modern medicine—psychiatry, in particular—advanced to where it is today…and all those today who don't have access to good health care.

Most important, I will feel rewarded if I'm able to reach those who haven't yet moved beyond trauma.

When I was a child, I remained helpless and mute but ever watchful of my mother in her torment. The shock treatments and tranquilizers available in the 1940s and '50s gave her temporary balance, but they robbed her of memory and diminished her dignity.

Most children in those years were not encouraged to ask questions. With no explanations for the behavior we witnessed, we lived with a fragile illusion of safety, an eggshell defense of protection. For me, that defense lasted until I reached adolescence, when hormones kicked in and brought me closer to becoming a woman and identifying with my mother. Only then did I begin to question my own stability, wondering whether any signs of anxiety or depression would lead to the kinds of catastrophic breakdowns that shook our home during our years in Brighton Beach, Brooklyn.

It wasn't until my twenties that I learned of my mother's earliest suicide attempt when *she* was in *her* twenties. The anesthesia of denial that had protected me then began to wear off, leaving me with an awareness that shifted from a mother I pitied to a self that I feared. Denying Mother's illness no longer served me. Love, loyalty, and despair conspired with the "dis-ease" that had crossed continents and joined generations. Shadows of her past fast became my nightmares, and unspoken family rules forced me to share in the losses and the pain of her life.

In order to confront my demons and not drown in my sorrows, the challenge for me was to learn to forgive—first my family and then myself. I reached out for professional guidance to break the family cycle of despair, and that's what I believe everyone in such circumstances must do eventually.

In my doing so, I learned to separate my mother from her illness and myself from my mother. Effective therapy gave me—as it can give others—a clearer context in which to store wounds. It didn't eradicate them, because the glimpses into places that no child should have to see, the acceptance of secrets and madness as being the norm, still color our lives despite how much we process the past.

If we could, we would prevent such images from intruding. At best, therapy teaches us that we're able to weaken their power by changing the lens through which we see them and reducing their size. At this safe distance, these images can no longer loom large enough to allow past events to trigger irrational responses in the present, poisoning our adult lives as they did our childhoods.

For me, it wasn't until I was married and had children that I was truly able to see how deeply affected I was by my childhood. Now, after more than thirty years as a psychotherapist, forty-six years as a wife, forty-four years as a mother, and thirteen years as a grand-mother, I hold on to the one belief I consider to be most valuable: the need to honor the parts of our selves that are healthy, the parts that are strong, even when unpredictable situations—our own physical or emotional stressors or those of our loved ones—catch us off guard.

Learning to accept my own dark side while honoring my strengths, I began to understand the healing power of forgiving and was more determined than ever to interrupt our family's dysfunction by merging life's sweetness with its sorrow, reconciling its meaning with its mystery.

Only then was I able to move beyond trauma—as I believe it is possible for others to do—with grace and dignity.

Linda Appleman Shapiro
July 2014

READING GROUP GUIDE

1. What does the title of the book mean to you?

2. How was Shapiro's childhood different from that of children in more normal households?

3. What traumas did Shapiro's mother experience as a child? How did hearing about them affect Shapiro?

4. What traumas did Shapiro experience as a child?

5. Have you had any personal experiences with mental illness with a family member or a friend? How do your personal experiences compare to Shapiro's experience?

6. Would you be able to recognize the signs of mental illness? Do you know any support services in your community that could be of help in such a situation?

7. Shapiro, her father, and her brother react differently to the mental illness of Shapiro's mother. Discuss their reactions and what each of them could have done differently.

8. Does the stigma of mental illness still exist? If so, what can be done to eliminate that stigma?

9. Do you think keeping family secrets is ever healthy? If so, when would it be appropriate to keep family secrets?

10. How do you feel about Herbie (Shapiro's older brother)? What did he do to help Shapiro? What more could he have done?

11. Shapiro talks about being "the girl" in an immigrant family, especially in the eyes of her father. Discuss the ways in which Shapiro's parents treated her and her brother differently.

12. Shapiro worries at various times in her life about being like her mother. In what ways is she similar to her mother? In what ways is she different? What does she do to help ensure that she will not suffer as she saw her mother suffer?

13. Shapiro talks about being "invisible" with her father, boyfriends, and others. Later, after becoming a psychotherapist and helping others, she says, "I am no longer invisible." What does she mean?

14. Do you believe it is possible to forgive and move beyond trauma without forgetting? Why or why not?

ABOUT DREAM OF THINGS

Dream of Things (dreamofthings.com) publishes memoirs, anthologies of creative nonfiction, and other books that fulfill our mission to publish distinctive voices and meaningful books. Other books from Dream of Things include:

Betty's Child
A Memoir by Donald R. Dempsey
A Hoffer Award Grand Prize Finalist.
"Heartrending and humorous." *Kirkus Review*

Swimming with Maya
A Mother's Story by Eleanor Vincent
"Vincent's poignant decision to donate Maya's organs will resonate with even hard-boiled readers." *Booklist*

Leaving the Hall Light On
A Mother's Memoir of Living with Her Son's Bipolar Disorder and Surviving His Suicide by Madeline Sharples
"A moving read of tragedy, trying to prevent it, and coping with life after." *Midwest Book Review*

Everything I Never Wanted to Be
A memoir of alcoholism and addiction, faith and family, hope and humor by Dina Kucera
"Raw and funny." Joel Stein, *Time Magazine* columnist
"Like a maelstrom." *ForeWord Review*

Daughters of Absence
Transforming a Legacy of Loss, ed. by Mindy Weisel
A collection of twelve essays written by daughters of Holocaust survivors.

Be There Now
Travel Stories from Around the World,
ed. by Julie Rand and Mike O'Mary
People sharing real stories of awe and insight, fear and laughter, humility and humanity as they explore the world around us.

Saying Goodbye
To the people, places and things in our lives,
ed. by Julie Rember and Mike O'Mary
"If you have ever had to deal with loss, read this book." *Midwest Book Review*

MFA in a Box
A Why to Write Book by John Rember
Winner of Hoffer, Nautilus and Midwest Book Awards.
"The essential truths about excellent writing." The Judges of the Hoffer Awards

The Note
A book about the power of appreciation by Mike O'Mary
Named Best Gift Book of 2011 in the Living Now Book Awards.

Wise Men and Other Stories
A collection of holiday-related stories by Mike O'Mary
Essays in the tradition of Robert Fulghum, Dave Barry, Bill Bryson, and other great American humorists.

ABOUT THE AUTHOR

Behavioral psychotherapist, oral historian, lecturer, and author, Linda Appleman Shapiro earned her B.A. in literature from Bennington College, a Master's degree in Human Development/ Counseling from the Bank Street College of Education, and a Master Certification in Neuro-Linguistic Programming from the New York Institute of N.L.P. She has further certifications in Ericksonian Hypnosis and Substance Abuse/Addictions Counseling.

Shapiro is a contributing author in the casebook, *Leaves Before the Wind: Leading Applications of N.L.P.*

In private practice for more than thirty years, Shapiro also served as a senior staff member at an out-patient facility for addicts and their families. As an oral historian, she has documented the lives of many of New York's elderly.

Her memoir, *Four Rooms, Upstairs*, was named Finalist in the Indie Next Generation Book Awards, and for her blog of three years, *A Psychotherapist's Journey*, Shapiro was named Top Blogger in the field of mental health by WELLsphere.

Married to actor and audiobook narrator George Guidall, Shapiro and her husband live in Westchester County, New York. They have two daughters and two grandchildren.

16441325R00152

Made in the USA
Middletown, DE
14 December 2014